CATHOLIC COLLECTIBLES

JUNE K. LAVAL

Photographs by Katherine Frye

4880 Lower Valley Road • Atglen, PA 19310

Other Schiffer books by June Laval:
Antique French Textiles for Designers, EAN 978-0-7643-2039-2

Other Schiffer books on related subjects:
Jewish Antiques: From Menorahs to Seltzer Bottles, by Tsadik Kaplan,
EAN 978-0-7643-4650-7

Designed by Molly Shields
Cover design by Danielle Farmer
Type set in Trajan Pro/Bodoni

ISBN: 978-0-7643-5146-4
Printed in China

Published by Schiffer Publishing, Ltd.
4880 Lower Valley Road
Atglen, PA 19310
Phone: (610) 593-1777; Fax: (610) 593-2002
E-mail: Info@schifferbooks.com
Web: www.schifferbooks.com

For our complete selection of fine books on this and related subjects,
please visit our website at www.schifferbooks.com. You may also write
for a free catalog.

Schiffer Publishing's titles are available at special discounts for bulk
purchases for sales promotions or premiums. Special editions, including
personalized covers, corporate imprints, and excerpts, can be created
in large quantities for special needs. For more information, contact the
publisher.

We are always looking for people to write books on new and related
subjects. If you have an idea for a book, please contact us at proposals@
schifferbooks.com.

To my husband, Philippe Laval.

Contents

FOREWORD

One thing that is definitely true about the Catholic Church is that it is mysterious and very spiritual. Most who enter a Catholic Church or attend the celebration of a Mass are caught up or at least impressed with the sense and spirit of mystery. The mystery of God's grace, His love and mercy, is the treasure of the Church! But it is a treasure very much held in earthen vessels. In the Church in the eighth and ninth centuries a controversy arose about the use of things: images, statues, any and all objects of pious devotion. By that time Christians were using all sorts of religious objects in many ways. Edicts were promulgated forbidding their use. However, people held on to these objects with absolute devotion. They refused to give them up. Religious objects of devotion are properly called icons. Eventually they were permitted and endorsed by the Church. Those who seek to destroy sacred images are called iconoclasts.

Religious articles and objects are outward and visible manifestations of inward and spiritual grace. Many people have pictures of loved ones or articles that belonged to people they love. We all have keepsakes: trophies from sporting events, certificates, diplomas, and even ticket stubs from rock concerts attended by devoted fans are kept and revered. Looking at them brings back memories and feelings. They are symbolic of deeper and more meaningful things.

Catholics, and indeed many Christians, make use of material religious things, but do not bow down and worship them. They use them to revere and worship what they signify, point us toward, and lead us to. They do not replace God the Father or His Son or His Holy Spirit, but they serve to enrich our experience of His Divine action in this world. Like most things they can be used for great good, but can also be abused if used improperly or for the wrong reason. The life and heritage of the Catholic Church is indeed rich and varied. It is anything but strictly and simply monolithic. This book illustrates this richness and variety of the Church in the present and the past, which can be seen in the incredible variety and diversity of objects pictured and discussed. Such objects, of course, stand on their own, but they also serve to broaden and deepen our experience of God. I think that is why they are fascinating, for the author and many of us.

Father David M. Dye
Administrator of Mary Our Queen parish
Atlanta Archdiocese

Acknowledgments

I would like to thank my dear colleague Dr. Lynn Fedeli, professor of Italian and Spanish at Kennesaw State University, for reading the manuscript and offering many helpful suggestions. My appreciation is also extended to Father David Dye, administrator of Mary Our Queen parish in the Atlanta Archdiocese, for his advice and helpful information on the Catholic Church, and for writing the foreword. He was kind enough to read the manuscript and give me additional information on the history of the objects in the book.

My visits to the Museum of Sacred Art (*Musée d'Art Sacré du Gard*) in Pont-Saint-Esprit, France, were of great help in the preparation of this book. I am particularly appreciative of the cooperation of Alain Girard, the curator of the museum. I highly recommend a visit to this museum in Provence to anyone interested in sacred art.

I also very much appreciate the assistance of the Interlibrary Loan office of the Sturgis Library at Kennesaw State University for searching high and low for books I needed in my research.

My greatest debt of appreciation goes to my husband, Philippe Laval, associate professor of mathematics at Kennesaw State University, and my personal computer guru, for his help and support at every stage in the writing of this book.

Photographs are courtesy of the author unless otherwise credited.

All objects pictured in this book are of French origin, unless otherwise indicated.

INTRODUCTION

Brief History of Christianity and Catholicism

According to Vatican figures, there are over a billion Catholics in the world today and they represent about one sixth of the world population. Catholics are Christians, and like Jews and Moslems they are monotheistic—they believe in one sole God. There are three important monotheistic religions in the world: Judaism, Christianity, and Islam. For Christians, the Bible is the Holy Book and the foundation of their faith. It is divided into two parts: the Old Testament and the New Testament. The Old Testament relates the history of the Jewish people and contains the Hebrew Scriptures. The New Testament tells the story of Jesus Christ, a Jew who, with the help of his apostles, spread the teachings of what became known as Christianity to many lands. Christians follow the teachings of Jesus Christ and believe that Jesus is part of the Holy Trinity: God the Father, Jesus the Son, and the Holy Spirit. These three entities form one.

The word *catholic* means universal, and for a long time Christians were united as Catholics. Then, in 1054, the Catholic Church split in two and was divided into the Western Church, known as the Roman Catholic Church, and the Eastern Church called the Orthodox Church (Greece, Ukraine, and Russia). One of the principle differences between the two is that the supreme authority of the Roman Catholic Church is the Pope while each Orthodox Church has its own spiritual leader known as the patriarch. In the worship service, there is the Western, or Latin, rite and the Eastern, or Byzantine, rite. The Church split again in the 1500s with the birth of Protestantism, which has many different denominations.

While the celebration of the Eucharist, or Mass, is the most essential part of Catholic worship, symbols and religious articles of devotion also occupy an important place in the veneration of God. Cathedrals and churches are filled with artistic treasures and works of art. Alongside this formal sacred art in churches are personal objects of worship that are more humble in nature and are found in the homes of the devoted. These personal articles of devotion, which may be worn by the faithful or displayed in prominent places in their homes, are the object of our study.

1800s crucifix with ebony inlay and skull and crossbones (*memento mori*) at foot of cross. 6" tall, $85–$95.

Three 1800s crucifixes with ebony inlay. 4½"–6" tall. $85–$125 each.

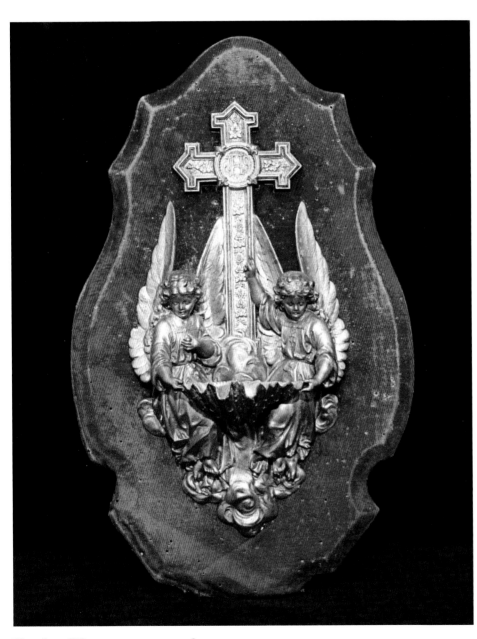

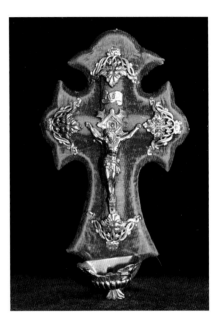

Napoleon III (circa 1870) red velvet crucifix with holy water font. 10" tall, $125–$150.

Napoleon III copper cross on red velvet with angels holding holy water font. 15" tall, $275–$300.

Napoleon III crucifix on blue velvet. Christ is made from carved bone. 14" tall, $135–$160.

Contemporary Guatemalan folk art crucifix on stand with tin nimbus. 9" tall, $60–$80.

Early-1900s carved wood crucifix with passion instruments on stand. 19" tall, $175–$225.

Early-1900s carved walnut crucifix with glass holy water font. 12" tall, $150–$195.

Early-1900s brass crucifix with shell-shaped font. 12" tall, $125–$150.

Contemporary shell cross with celluloid Christ on three-tiered stand. 10" tall, $75–$95.

Two art nouveau silver-on-copper plaques on stand from Lourdes shrine. *Left*: 4" tall, $50–$60. *Right*: 5½" tall, $75–$85.

Early-1900s bronze statue of Joseph holding Christ Child. 8" tall, $95–$125.

Early-1900s Sacred Heart of Mary plaque framed in blue glass. 9½" in diameter, $95–$125.

Early-1900s mother of pearl holy water font from Lourdes shrine with the Virgin Mary and filigree border. 6" tall, $85–$100.

Early-1900s framed Saint Thérèse marble plaque with glass holy water font. 7" tall, $149–$160.

Personal Objects of Devotion

This book is intended to be an introduction and practical guide to the history and appreciation of common, everyday devotional objects—those we find in the home that are destined for daily use, display, and inspiration. They are personal items of piety that often are handed down from generation to generation. This book is meant to be only an introduction for those who would like to know more about these articles. It is not directed exclusively to Catholics, and attempts to offer basic information to anyone who is curious about the objects' history and origins. It is also written for collectors who are attracted to these inspiring personal objects of veneration. The images and values of these numerous articles will help show the beauty, originality, and variety of these objects. Since they were manufactured for the general public from all walks of life and social status, rich and poor, these items were never expensive. They were sold at pilgrimage sites, outside churches by both men and women, in small shops, and by traveling salesmen. Most of the articles we find on the market today are from the time span of the 1880s to the 1960s. Their popularity began to decline after World War II and production began to taper off after the 1960s. Once again there is a demand for these objects, and they are still reasonable in price. The market value for most of these articles is under $200. The articles shown in the book are antique or vintage and are beautiful and well made. Mass-produced religious articles made in China are not shown. Our goal is to give basic information on objects of piety that are still used and appreciated by those who search for them. We will explore popular devotional art of the past created by local artisans in towns and villages as well as in small factories in major cities. Since France produced an enormous amount of these sacred objects and they are readily available at reasonable prices in the marketplace, we will feature many articles from France.

Early-1900s Our Lady of Fourvière enamel image on brass plaque. 6" tall, $125–$150.

Early-1900s brass statue of the Infant of Prague. 5" tall, $95–$125.

Today there is a renewed interest in objects of devotion. These objects are the key to an intimate understanding of the spiritual past and of the people who are not in the history books. Whether the object is elaborate or humble, the function is the same: to connect heaven and earth, the world we live in with the invisible world that is only accessible through faith. It is important to understand that these articles of personal devotion represent symbols only and are not objects of worship. We are indebted to William Worth, who pointed out the clear explanation of this idea expressed by Fray Maturino in Colonial times (Worth, 1998, 161). In the sixteenth century Fray Maturino Gilberti, a Franciscan monk in Mexico, explained this concept to the Tarascan Indians:

> We do not worship any image, even though it be that of the Crucifix or St. Mary, for, when we represent the Crucifix or St. Mary or the Saints, it is only to remind ourselves of the great mercy of God, who gave us His Son for our redemption, and . . . although we kneel before the Crucifix in an attitude of worship, it is nevertheless not the Crucifix that we worship, for it is only made of wood, but God Himself, Our Lord who is in Heaven. (Ricard, 1966, 103)

In past times the object itself was part of religious obligations. Today this function is still present but the scope of the object goes even further. These objects appeal to a wider public through their beauty, their spirituality, their personality, and their originality.

Early-1900s copper church on stand with picture of Saint Thérèse inside. 3½" tall, $75–$85.

Early-1900s wood rosary with sixty Ave Maria beads and large wooden cross. 89" long, $125–$145.

Early-1900s crystal rosary with sterling silver cross. 34" long, $85–$100.

This book is in no way an in-depth study of religion or theology. The religious objects we will study are more a part of culture than theology. For example, in the past, praying the rosary was a part of a daily routine for most practicing Catholics. Sometimes it was prayed regularly as a family activity or the rosary was kept in a little pouch so as to be close at hand for prayer during the day. Crosses and holy water fonts were a common part of the décor of most homes, sometimes the only adornment in the home. Crucifixes were commonly hung over the bed in many Catholic homes. Large crucifixes were placed at the entrances and exits of villages, on rural roads, and in cemeteries. Just as they still are today, crosses and religious medals were worn around the neck as a sign of religious belief. Ex-votos are religious paintings that give thanks for a miracle or a favor received and show the story of how a divine being saved a person who invoked help; they also often show interiors of the home and details of how people lived in the past. Objects of piety give us valuable insight into the people and their beliefs. These objects still inspire people and give comfort and solace to the faithful. They are also seen as articles of protection from accidents, fire, death, and illness, as well as symbols of hope in difficult times. The saints have certain miraculous attributes and are called upon for help in emergencies and strife.

Early-1900s bronze crucifix with Mary and Joseph and skull and crossbones at the foot on a three-tiered stand. 7" tall, $85–$115.

Early-1900s silver medallion of the Virgin Mary on a marble plaque signed by the engraver. 4" square, $75–$95.

Early-1900s enamel portrait of Saint Anne d'Auray in brass frame. 5" tall, $125–$150.

Early-1900s silk figures from a church banner showing Saint Anne with the young Virgin Mary. 15" tall, $85–$115.

Early-1900s silk figure from a church banner showing the Virgin Mary holding a rosary. 14" tall, $85–$115.

Rosewood rosary dated 1858, with 150 Ave Maria beads. One side of the heart says "I am the Immaculate Conception,"; the other side gives the date 1858. $250–$300.

Two early-1900s small leather pouches with rosaries inside. $65–$75 each.

Early-1900s brass Virgin Mary with
Christ Child with holy water font at the
base on walnut plaque. 8" × 15",
$175–$225.

Early-1900s framed copper crucifix on
red moiré background. 12" × 17",
$150–$175.

1938 Mexican retablo (ex-voto), Remualda Ordoñes gives thanks to the Virgin of Guadalupe for saving her husband. 12 ½" × 9", $125–$150.

1931 Mexican retablo, Lucia Arizmendi gives thanks to the Virgin of Zapopan for the return of her son after he fell in with a bad crowd. 13" × 9", $125–$150.

1931 Mexican retablo, A hunter gives thanks to the Virgin of Guadalupe for saving him from a tiger when he was hunting in the mountains. 11" × 8", $125–$150.

Early-1900s copper heart with seven daggers representing the seven sorrows of the Virgin Mary. 12" × 12", $150–$175.

Early-1900s white marble holy water font with marble cross and grape leaves. 5" × 8", $200–$250.

People feel a closeness and devotion to certain popular saints and holy people. Our Lady of Lourdes appears in every kind of object imaginable, even lamps that double as music boxes. Her medal is one of the most popular medals produced. Saint Christopher, even though he no longer appears on the liturgical calendar, is still popular with travelers who wear his medal or carry a key chain with his image. Often police officers and soldiers wear a medal of Saint Michael for protection. Each saint and holy being has special attributes and symbols. For example, the mother pelican feeding her young with her own blood is a symbol of Christ's sacrifice of his own life. The lily is a symbol of the purity of the Virgin Mary. A beautiful and complicated Saint Benedict medal has initials of messages in Latin and is worn to keep the wearer safe and to ward off evil. Saint Joseph and Saint Anthony of Padua are often pictured with the Christ Child. Our Lady of Mount Carmel holds Jesus as a child with a scapular. Rosaries are still a part of daily devotion. Medals with a favorite saint are often worn for protection or special devotion. The biographies of saints fill many books since there are thousands of them. The compilations of their stories are known as hagiographies and are still being published today. All of these articles of beauty and reverence fill a spiritual need for many of the faithful.

Early-1900s image of the apparition of the Virgin Mary at Lourdes under convex glass. It is also a thermometer. 4" × 5", $45–$50.

Art nouveau copper plaque on stand with picture of Saint Thérèse. 2" × 4", $35–$45.

Art deco metal music box representing the apparition of the Virgin Mary at Lourdes. The music box plays "Ave Maria." 8" tall, $50–$75.

Early-1900s lamp with pink roses representing the apparition of the Virgin Mary at Lourdes. The lamp also plays "Ave Maria." 6" tall, $50–$75.

Early-1900s brass plaque on stand with the Virgin Mary and Christ Child. 2" × 3", $35–$45.

Art nouveau bronze wall plaque representing the Immaculate Conception. 4" tall, $50–$75.

Early-1900s copper medallion of Saint Thérèse, signed by the engraver. 3" in diameter, $35–$45.

Early-1900s oval brass framed picture of Saint Anthony. 2 ½" × 4", $35–$45.

Contemporary pewter cross with a modern Virgin Mary and Christ child, surrounded by praying figures. 6" tall, $50–$60.

Early-1900s brass medallion of the Virgin Mary and Christ child. 3" in diameter, $35–$45.

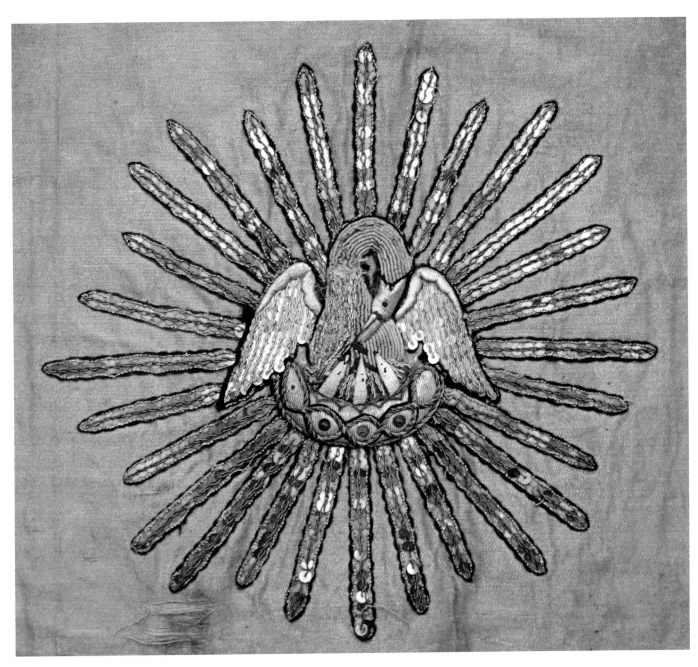

Early-1900s detail of pelican feeding her
young. Image from ecclesiastical garment with
rich couching and sequins. $300–$350.

CHAPTER ONE

THE ROSARY

Definition

The word *rosary* comes from the Latin *rosarium*, which means rose garden. It also means a garland or bouquet of roses. There is also the idea of a crown, or *chapelet*, associated with the word *rosarium*. Roses have always been associated with the Virgin Mary and the Virgin of Guadalupe, as well as with saints such as Saint Thérèse of Lisieux and Saint Rose of Lima, who are always portrayed with roses. A beautiful legend that circulated all over Europe in ancient times tells of a young monk who was reciting the rosary when the Virgin appeared to him and took rosebuds from his mouth and wove them to form a garland that she placed on her head (Thurston and Shipman, 1912). The word *bead* comes from the Anglo-Saxon *bede*, which meant prayer. Long ago the large beads of the rosary were called roses because they were made from small dried fruit coming from the East, which looked like tiny flowers (Stampfler, 2011, 11). Even today some rosaries have wood beads carved to resemble rose buds.

The rosary is a practical instrument of prayer. It represents a daily practice of devotion and is a prayer of the people, used by the educated and the uneducated, the wealthy and the poor. The rosary is a treasure of devotion and piety and the word refers to the meditation and prayers that accompany its recitation as well as to the beads used to pray. The modern rosary is an orderly guide to meditation and prayers. Most rosaries in modern times have fifty-nine beads. Most beads are in groups of ten, which are called decades. One says a Hail Mary for each bead. A few beads are isolated and correspond to the Our Father prayer. See the illustration for a more detailed explanation of how to recite the rosary. The Hail Mary is the greeting to the Virgin Mary by the Archangel Gabriel when he visited her to announce the birth of Christ. In Luke 1:28 in the New Testament we read: "And the angel came unto her, and said, Hail thou that art highly favored, the Lord is with thee: blessed art thou among women." Later Mary went to visit her cousin Elizabeth who said to her: "Blessed art thou among women, and blessed is the fruit of thy womb" (Luke 1:42). In the

Early-1900s framed enamel pin of Saint Thérèse holding roses. 1½" in diameter, $35–$45.

Three early-1900s Saint Thérèse medals. 1" tall, $40–$50 each.

Late-1800s carved ivory rosary. Ebony inlay crucifix has skull and crossbones at the foot of the cross. 52" long, $250–$275.

Late-1800s rosary with brass heart and 150 Ave Maria beads. $200–$250.

fifteenth century the second part of the Hail Mary was added by Saint Bernardine of Siena, a Franciscan priest: "Holy Mary, Mother of God, pray for us sinners" and at the end of the fifteenth century the words "now and at the hour of our death" were added (Berthod, 2006, 67). The Lord's Prayer, which Jesus taught his disciples, is found in Matthew 6:9-13 as well as in Luke 11:2-4. Although the number of prayers to be recited in a rosary may seem daunting, it takes at most twenty minutes for those who are accustomed to praying the rosary on a daily basis. For many, saying the rosary is a form of solace and inspiration. The rosary we will study is the rosary of the Western Church.

Early-1900s jasper rosary. 36" long, $95–$135.

Early-1900s brown enamel rosary with reliquary crucifix. 39" long, $75–$95.

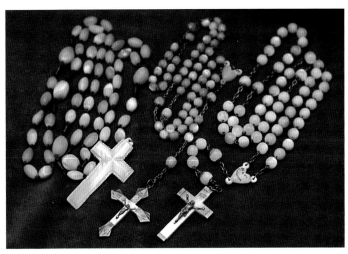

Three early-1900s mother of pearl rosaries. 34" – 40" long, $100–$150 each.

Four early-1900s colored glass bead rosaries with silver crucifixes. 29"–35" long, $95–$125 each.

Late-1800s porcelain rosary; heart has "Holy Spirit" on both sides. 37" long, $100 -$125.

Late-1800s mother of pearl rosary with large beads in original blue satin box. Heart reads "Souvenir de 1ère Communion." 45" long, $275–$325.

Origins and History of the Rosary

There are several theories about the origins of the rosary. One theory attributes its origin to Saint Dominic in the thirteenth century during the Albigensian heresy in Southwestern France. The Albigensians denied the doctrine of the Incarnation of God through His Son, Jesus. Saint Dominic sought the help of the Virgin Mary during this difficult conflict and was advised by her to preach the rosary among the people as "an antidote to heresy and sin." Saint Dominic is associated with the rosary because he popularized it by spreading the word of its importance to the masses through his sermons.

Another more plausible theory is that the use of pebbles, beads, or seeds gathered in a pouch or perhaps threaded on a string as a guide to meditation and prayer developed over a long period of time. The use of such beads dates from very early times and was present in many religions and cultures. It is thought that the rosary was inspired by the 150 biblical Psalms that the monks and nuns were required to pray. Thus the early rosaries had 150 beads. The rosary as we know it developed over time to be used by the faithful who could not read and desired to express their devotion to Jesus and Mary with memorized prayers. The beads were eventually strung together to make it easier to pray and at the same time keep the faithful focused on their meditation and prayers while avoiding distraction. At first these early rosaries were a series of repetitions of the Lord's Prayer, thus the name in Latin *Paternoster* (Our Father). The manufacturers of these strings of beads were called *paternosterers*. As early as the thirteenth century there were craft guilds for these artisans. These strings of prayer beads came into use before the Hail Mary or Ave Maria beads and prayers, and it was not until they were already a popular devotional article that the Marian rosary came into use. Eventually the *paternosters* and the Marian rosaries were united into one object of devotion: the rosary as we know it today. All of this is the result of developments over several centuries.

Detail of the rosary in the previous picture.

Early-1900s finger rosary inscribed "Ave Maria." $45–$55.

Bracelet made from broken coral
rosary beads and bronze religious
medals. $150-$195.

1900s finger rosary. $40–$50.

Early-1900s brown enamel rosary with ten
religious medals. 36" long, $125–$145.

An important event in the history of the development of the popularity of the rosary happened during the Battle of Lepanto in the sixteenth century. Don Juan de Austria, half-brother of King Phillip II of Spain, led a fleet to attack Moslem forces in Lepanto, Turkey. Pope Pius V urged the faithful to pray to the Virgin Mary for victory in the battle and to pray the rosary. The Virgin Mary appeared as Our Lady of Victory, also known as the Virgin of the Rosary. Since that day, the Feast of the Holy Rosary has been celebrated on October 7 and is a holy day on the liturgical calendar. Although the Christians were outnumbered in both ships and men, they defeated the enemy on October 7, 1571. The most famous soldier in that battle was the illustrious Miguel de Cervantes y Saavedra, who in 1605 would publish the first part of his novel *Don Quixote de la Mancha*. As a result of an injury in that battle, Cervantes lost the use of his left arm and was thereafter known as *El Manco de Lepanto*, the "One-armed Man of Lepanto." Unfortunately, on his way back to Spain, his ship was captured by pirates and he spent seven years in captivity in Algeria waiting for someone to pay his ransom. He was finally rescued by the Mercerian fathers, who dedicated themselves to raising money to pay the ransom for travelers captured by pirates at sea.

Left: Late-1800s mother of pearl rosary with mother of pearl crucifix. 36" long, $125–$175.
Right: Mother of pearl rosary bracelet with large mother of pearl beads and two silver First Communion medals. 10" long, $125–$175.

Holy card from rue Saint Sulpice in Paris, showing Our Lady of Victory (Our Lady of the Rosary). $6–$7.

The form of the rosary remained the same for a long time after its creation until the early fifteenth century when a Cartusian monk named Henry Kalkar divided the 150 Hail Marys into decades (sets of ten) separated by Our Fathers. Not long after that, Hail Marys were separated into five decades, thus resembling the rosaries we find today. The rosary is used not only to pray but also to contemplate mysteries. There were originally fifteen mysteries, standardized in the sixteenth century by Pope Pius VI. In 2002 Pope John Paul II announced five new optional mysteries, called the Luminous mysteries,

Early-1900s boxwood rosary with 150 small beads. 74" long, $75–$85.

1900s carved wood monk's rosary with beads joined with rope. 104" long, $85–$125.

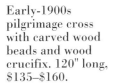

Early-1900s pilgrimage cross with carved wood beads and wood crucifix. 120" long, $135–$160.

for a total of twenty mysteries. (See "How to recite the Holy Rosary," page 32, for an explanation.) The mysteries are the stories of events in the life of Christ and the contemplation of their meaning. Examples are: Jesus in the temple, His baptism in the river Jordan, and the crucifixion and resurrection. There are also other optional prayers that go along with the rosary such as the Fatima Prayer at the end of each decade. This was added in the twentieth century. The Rosary Novena is the praying of the rosary on nine consecutive days.

Two early-1900s carved bone rosaries that have crosses with pictures inside the round openings. 26"–30" long, $75–$90 each.

World War I soldier's cross with national colors of France and silver cross. 18" long, $45–$55.

Early-1900s mother of pearl necklace made from broken rosary beads and mother of pearl crucifixes. 30" long, $295–$350.

How to Recite the Holy Rosary

1. SAY THESE PRAYERS...

IN THE NAME of the Father, and of the Son, and of the Holy Spirit. Amen. *(As you say this, with your right hand touch your forehead when you say* Father, *touch your breastbone when you say* Son, *touch your left shoulder when you say* Holy, *and touch your right shoulder when you say* Spirit.*)*

I BELIEVE IN GOD, the Father almighty, Creator of Heaven and earth. And in Jesus Christ, His only Son, our Lord, Who was conceived by the Holy Spirit, born of the Virgin Mary, suffered under Pontius Pilate; was crucified, died, and was buried. He descended into Hell. The third day He rose again from the dead. He ascended into Heaven, and sits at the right hand of God, the Father almighty. He shall come again to judge the living and the dead. I believe in the Holy Spirit, the holy Catholic Church, the communion of saints, the forgiveness of sins, the resurrection of the body, and life everlasting. Amen.

OUR FATHER, Who art in Heaven, hallowed be Thy Name. Thy kingdom come, Thy will be done on earth as it is in Heaven. Give us this day our daily bread, and forgive us our trespasses, as we forgive those who trespass against us. And lead us not into temptation, but deliver us from evil. Amen.

HAIL MARY, full of grace, the Lord is with thee. Blessed art thou among women, and blessed is the fruit of thy womb, Jesus. Holy Mary, Mother of God, pray for us sinners, now and at the hour of our death. Amen.

GLORY BE to the Father, and to the Son, and to the Holy Spirit. As it was in the beginning is now, and ever shall be, world without end. Amen.

O MY JESUS, forgive us our sins, save us from the fires of Hell; lead all souls to Heaven, especially those in most need of Thy mercy. Amen.

HAIL HOLY QUEEN, mother of mercy; our life, our sweetness, and our hope. To thee do we cry, poor banished children of Eve. To thee do we send up our sighs, mourning and weeping in this vale of tears. Turn, then, most gracious advocate, thine eyes of mercy toward us. And after this, our exile, show unto us the blessed fruit of thy womb, Jesus. O clement, O loving, O sweet Virgin Mary. Pray for us, O holy Mother of God, that we may be made worthy of the promises of Christ. Amen.

O GOD, WHOSE only-begotten Son by His life, death and resurrection, has purchased for us the rewards of eternal life; grant, we beseech Thee, that by meditating upon these mysteries of the Most Holy Rosary of the Blessed Virgin Mary, we may imitate what they contain and obtain what they promise, through the same Christ our Lord. Amen.

ANNOUNCE *each mystery by saying something like, "The third Joyful Mystery is the Birth of Our Lord." This is required only when saying the Rosary in a group.*

2. IN THIS ORDER...

INTRODUCTION
1. IN THE NAME...
2. I BELIEVE IN GOD...
3. OUR FATHER...
4. HAIL MARY...
5. HAIL MARY...
6. HAIL MARY...
7. GLORY BE...
8. O MY JESUS...

THE FIRST DECADE
9. ANNOUNCE...
10. OUR FATHER...
11. HAIL MARY...
12. HAIL MARY...
13. HAIL MARY...
14. HAIL MARY...
15. HAIL MARY...
16. HAIL MARY...
17. HAIL MARY...
18. HAIL MARY...
19. HAIL MARY...
20. HAIL MARY...
21. GLORY BE...
22. O MY JESUS...

THE SECOND DECADE
23. ANNOUNCE...
24. OUR FATHER...
25. HAIL MARY...
26. HAIL MARY...
27. HAIL MARY...
28. HAIL MARY...
29. HAIL MARY...
30. HAIL MARY...
31. HAIL MARY...
32. HAIL MARY...
33. HAIL MARY...
34. HAIL MARY...
35. GLORY BE...
36. O MY JESUS...

THE THIRD DECADE
37. ANNOUNCE...
38. OUR FATHER...
39. HAIL MARY...
40. HAIL MARY...
41. HAIL MARY...
42. HAIL MARY...
43. HAIL MARY...
44. HAIL MARY...
45. HAIL MARY...
46. HAIL MARY...
47. HAIL MARY...
48. HAIL MARY...
49. GLORY BE...
50. O MY JESUS...

THE FOURTH DECADE
51. ANNOUNCE...
52. OUR FATHER...
53. HAIL MARY...
54. HAIL MARY...
55. HAIL MARY...
56. HAIL MARY...
57. HAIL MARY...
58. HAIL MARY...
59. HAIL MARY...
60. HAIL MARY...
61. HAIL MARY...
62. HAIL MARY...
63. GLORY BE...
64. O MY JESUS...

THE FIFTH DECADE
65. ANNOUNCE...
66. OUR FATHER...
67. HAIL MARY...
68. HAIL MARY...
69. HAIL MARY...
70. HAIL MARY...
71. HAIL MARY...
72. HAIL MARY...
73. HAIL MARY...
74. HAIL MARY...
75. HAIL MARY...
76. HAIL MARY...
77. GLORY BE...
78. O MY JESUS...

CONCLUSION
79. HAIL HOLY QUEEN...
80. O GOD, WHOSE...
81. IN THE NAME...

3. WHILE TOUCHING THESE BEADS TO KEEP TRACK OF YOUR PROGRESS...

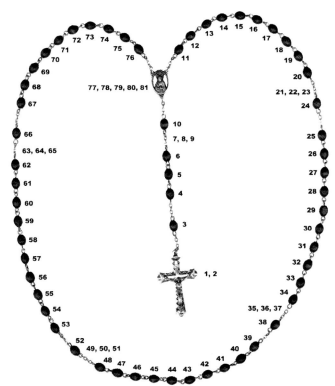

4. AND SILENTLY MEDITATING ON THESE "MYSTERIES", OR EVENTS FROM THE LIVES OF JESUS AND MARY...

On Monday and Saturday, meditate on the "Joyful Mysteries"
First Decade (Steps 9-22): The Annunciation of Gabriel to Mary (Luke 1:26-38)
Second Decade (Steps 23-36): The Visitation of Mary to Elizabeth (Luke 1:39-56)
Third Decade (Steps 37-50): The Birth of Our Lord (Luke 2:1-21)
Fourth Decade (Steps 51-64): The Presentation of Our Lord (Luke 2:22-38)
Fifth Decade (Steps 65-78): The Finding of Our Lord in the Temple (Luke 2:41-52)

On Thursday, meditate on the "Luminous Mysteries"
First Decade: The Baptism of Our Lord in the River Jordan (Matthew 3:13-16)
Second Decade: The Wedding at Cana, when Christ manifested Himself (Jn 2:1-11)
Third Decade: The Proclamation of the Kingdom of God (Mark 1:14-15)
Fourth Decade: The Transfiguration of Our Lord (Matthew 17:1-8)
Fifth Decade: The Last Supper, when Our Lord gave us the Holy Eucharist (Mt 26)

On Tuesday and Friday, meditate on the "Sorrowful Mysteries"
First Decade: The Agony of Our Lord in the Garden (Matthew 26:36-56)
Second Decade: Our Lord is Scourged at the Pillar (Matthew 27:26)
Third Decade: Our Lord is Crowned with Thorns (Matthew 27:27-31)
Fourth Decade: Our Lord Carries the Cross to Calvary (Matthew 27:32)
Fifth Decade: The Crucifixion of Our Lord (Matthew 27:33-56)

On Wednesday and Sunday, meditate on the "Glorious Mysteries"
First Decade: The Glorious Resurrection of Our Lord (John 20:1-29)
Second Decade: The Ascension of Our Lord (Luke 24:36-53)
Third Decade: The Descent of the Holy Spirit at Pentecost (Acts 2:1-41)
Fourth Decade: The Assumption of Mary into Heaven
Fifth Decade: The Coronation of Mary as Queen of Heaven and Earth

You are encouraged to copy and distribute this sheet.

www.newadvent.org

Guide to praying the rosary.

The Scapular

The wearing of the scapular often accompanies the praying of the rosary. The word *scapular* comes from the Latin *scapula*, or shoulder. The scapular is an article of clothing worn over the shoulders by numerous religious orders. It is composed of two large bands of fabric that fall over the front and back of the religious garment. Its abbreviated form consists of two small pieces of cloth that each have a religious image (often the Virgin Mary) and are held together by two long ribbons or cords. It can also be a single image worn around the neck on a ribbon. These scapulars are often seen in religious processions. The form of the scapular is always square or rectangle, never round or oval, and is made of different colors depending on the religious order represented. For example, the scapular of Our Lady of Mount Carmel (the Carmelite order) must be of a dark color, usually brown (the word *carmelita* means brown in Cuba and Chile), while the blue scapular signifies the order of the Immaculate Conception.

The scapular is not fixed to the garment but rather is designed to hang from the neck or to be worn over the shoulders, front and back. Sometimes the scapular is worn

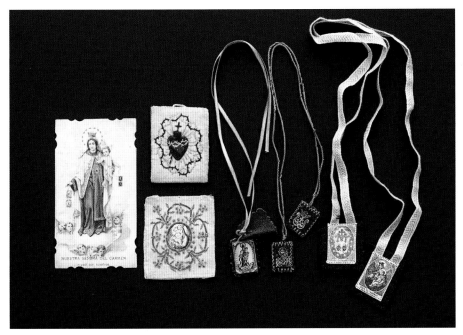

1886 holy card showing Our Lady of Carmel (Carmen) with the Christ child, both holding Carmelite scapulars. $6–$7. Assorted small scapulars, $20–$25 each.

Sheet of Our Lady of La Salette scapular engravings published in the late-1800s by Ouvry in Ambert, France. Sheet of seventy-two images to be made into scapulars. $75–$100 a sheet.

Sheet of Our Lady of Lourdes scapular engravings published in the late 1800s by Ouvry in Ambert, France. Sheet of seventy-two images to be made into scapulars. $75–$100 a sheet.

Sheet of Our Lady of Carmel and Sacred Hearts of Jesus, Mary, and Joseph scapular engravings published in the late 1800s by Ouvry in Ambert, France. Sheet of thirty-six images to be made into scapulars. $75–$100 a sheet.

under clothing. The scapular is a symbol of devotion and faith and is often worn by lay persons. It is an article of protection and is said to save the wearer from harm. In 1910, Pope Pius X authorized the replacement of the scapular with a religious medal. This is the reason the Virgin of Carmel is shown with the Christ Child who is holding a scapular that almost looks like a purse with strings. This image is frequently seen on the reverse side of Sacred Heart medals.

The scapular should be blessed and placed on the wearer in a special ceremony. According to the account of Lucia Santos, one of the three children who witnessed the apparition of the Virgin Mary in Fatima, Portugal, the Virgin said, "The rosary and the scapular are inseparable." The scapular continues to be an important object of devotion and a visible symbol of faith. During the Cristero civil wars in Mexico in the 1920s, the wearing of the scapular by a devout Catholic could mean death if caught by the opposing government faction.

Early-1900s figure from a church banner showing Our Lady of Carmel with the Christ child, each holding scapulars. 19" tall, $125–$140.

Early-1900s brass medallion showing Our Lady of Carmel with the Christ child, each holding scapulars and surrounded by angels. Initialed by the engraver. 6½" in diameter, $60–$90.

Early-1900s brass medallion showing Our Lady of Carmel with the Christ child holding scapulars. Initialed by the engraver. 6½" in diameter, $60–$90.

Early-1900s brass medallion showing Our Lady of Carmel with the Christ Child holding scapulars. Initialed by the engraver. 6½" in diameter, $60–$90.

Four early-1900s religious medals showing Our Lady of Carmel with the Christ child, each holding scapulars. ¾"–1½" in diameter, $45–$55 each.

In the past the rosary was a constant companion of the devout. It could easily be slipped into a pocket to be used during the day. Sometimes long rosaries were worn tied around the waist in some religious orders. The rosary continues to be an important instrument of prayer in the Catholic Church. In addition to its spiritual attributes, the value of the rosary itself as an object of beauty is not to be underestimated. Rosaries are made of a myriad of materials, from the very simple such as wood, seeds, glass, or even plastic to the more opulent, using ivory, mother of pearl, or precious stones such as amethysts, garnets, agate, tiger's eye, and lapis lazuli, just to mention a few. Mother of pearl rosaries are among the most popular today. They are used as gifts to commemorate special occasions such as baptism, First Communion, and marriage, and are to be treasured as personal objects of devotion by generations to come.

The older, beautifully made rosaries are most in demand, especially those from the 1800s. There are very few rosaries available from earlier centuries. Many rosaries have been broken or have lost a few beads. Often the cross on the rosary comes off and becomes separated from the beads. Rosaries must be blessed in order to be used for prayer. A blessed rosary can be lent, given as a gift or inherited (Stampfler, 2011, 51). If a rosary that has been blessed is destroyed or is missing more than four or five

beads, or if it has been sold to a third party, it is no longer considered blessed. Rosaries as well as religious medals must be buried, never thrown away. One reason very old rosaries are scarce is that often people were buried with a rosary clasped in their hands. Another reason for the scarcity of antique rosaries is that the very special rosaries are in private collections.

Six early-1900s rosary cases with small rosaries inside. 1"–2" in diameter, $40–$50 each.

Early-1900s mother of pearl case with 29" rosary inside. The case is 3½" long. $75–$100.

Five early-1900s tiny oval-shaped rosary cases with rosaries inside. 1"– 2", $40–$60 each.

Four early-1900s blue rosary bracelets commemorating the First Communion. 9"–11", $75–$100 each.

Left: Early-1900s pink quartz First Communion rosary with sterling crucifix. 43" long, $125–$145, *Right*: Matching First Communion rosary bracelet with First Communion medals, 10" long, $85–$100.

Early-1900s chromolithograph of the apparition of the Virgin Mary at Lourdes. Bernadette offers a rosary to the Virgin. 8" × 10", $35–$45.

Tiny leather purse with coral rosary inside. 20", $50–$60.

Early-1900s grouping of small leather pouches used to carry rosaries. 1½"–3", $10–$20 each.

William Edwards, seven years old, learning to say the rosary and understand its meaning. His first grade class at Our Lady of the Assumption in Atlanta, Georgia, made this rosary themselves with the help of their teacher, Ms. Janet Jovert.

Late-1800s rosary with 150 carved olive seed beads. 140" long, $135–$160.

Three early-1900s holy cards showing rosaries used at a First Communion ceremony. $6–$7 each.

Mid-1900s five-continents rosaries. The five different colors represent Africa (green), America (red), Europe (white), Oceana (blue), and Asia (yellow). 16"–37", $45–$60 each.

CHAPTER TWO

CROSSES AND CRUCIFIXES

History of the Cross in the Christian World

The cross, an instrument of death in the punishment of Christ, is the most famous symbol of the Christian faith. The word *cross* comes from the Latin word *crux* and is a juxtaposition of two lines that cross at right angles. For the Romans, the cross represented a material instrument of punishment and did not have a symbolic meaning. However what later became the symbol of Christianity did not originate with the death of Christ but rather had ancient beginnings in both the East and the West and was used by other cultures before the birth of Christ. Even in the earliest times the cross had a symbolic religious meaning. Orazio Marucchi, in his article "Archaeology of the Cross and the Crucifix" in *The Catholic Encyclopedia*, explains the origins of the cross in other civilizations and gives a clear explanation of the history of the cross and the crucifix in the Christian world (Marucchi, 1908). There are more than 400 versions of the cross but only about fifty of these are commonly used in Christian symbolism and decoration (Webber, 1971, 99). However, most of these variations are derived from the four basic forms of the cross. The equilateral or Greek cross has the transverse beam half way up the vertical beam. This is the cross used by the Red Cross. The Latin cross has a horizontal bar shorter than the vertical bar. Another kind of cross is the Tau cross of Egyptian origin, shaped like a T. This cross is also referred to as Saint Anthony's cross because it is said he wore such a cross on his robe. Yet another cross is one shaped like an X, which is the symbol for the Roman numeral ten as well as the Greek letter *chi*. It is called the Saint Andrew's cross because this saint is said to have suffered martyrdom on this cross. When the Greek letters *chi* (X) and *rho* (P) are superimposed they form the abbreviation of the name Christos, Christ.

Early-1900s tau cross with carved bone Christ (shepherd's cross). 13" tall, $75–$100.

Three 1900s tau crosses. $40–$60 each.

Amethyst cross ring. $125–$150.

Early-1900s Latin cross on stand.
20" tall, $100–$125.

The cross where Jesus died was a Latin or Roman cross (*crux immissa*) (Marucchi, 1908). The vertical pole is called the *stipes* and the transversal pole is the *patibulum*. In the Latin cross the transverse beam is about two-thirds of the way up the vertical beam. Each pole was made from a solid piece of resistant wood, possibly oak or cedar, but not from olive wood as it is not strong enough to support the weight of a man (De Landsburg, 2001, 11). This is the most common form of the cross.

During the first two centuries of Christianity the use of the cross as a symbol was rare because of its reference to such a degrading and humiliating method of public execution, high on a hill for all to witness as a sort of spectacle. In addition, this terrible symbol could have been detrimental and even dangerous to the new religion and perhaps hinder its development. Religious persecution was a constant danger for the early Christians as the large number of martyrs will attest. The cross became more common as a symbol during the fourth century. Instrumental in its acceptance was Helena, the mother of Emperor Constantine, the first Christian emperor of the Roman Empire. Early in the fourth century Helena converted to Christianity. Her son Constantine had granted freedom of worship to the Christians in 313 with the edict of Milan. In 326, at the age of eighty, tradition has it that she made a pilgrimage to Jerusalem where she discovered remains

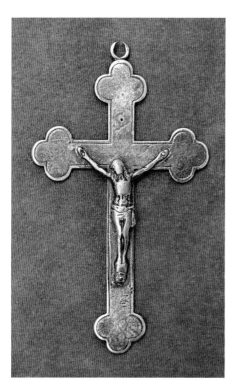

Late-1800s nun's profession silver crucifix with "fille de Marie immaculée" and image of the Virgin engraved on the reverse side. 3" tall, $95–$125.

Late-1800s wood crucifix with fleur-de-lys ends and thorns. 18" tall, $145–$175.

1930s crucifix with metal art deco designs on ends of cross. 14" tall, $75–$115.

Early-1900s brass crucifix with Matthew, Mark, Luke, and John images and symbols on ends of cross. 4" tall, $75–$100.

1800s *croix des vachers* (cattlemen's cross) near Salers, in the Auvergne region of France.

Art deco crucifix on metal stand with passion instruments. 16" tall, $125–$175.

of the True Cross, which had been carefully hidden after the death of Christ. According to tradition, the Jews had buried the cross and covered it over with stones. It is said that three crosses were found but the cross upon which Jesus died was revealed through a miracle. Helena sent pieces of this cross to many important places and she and Constantine erected a basilica over the Holy Sepulcher in Jerusalem. The basilica, named St. Constantinus, was later destroyed by the Persians. Helena also brought a piece of the True Cross to Constantine in Rome. In 635, what was left of the cross was sent to Constantinople (today Istanbul), where it was placed in the church of Saint Sophia. The Roman Emperor converted officially to the Christian religion the year he died, 337. The cross was important for him as well as for his mother. According to legend, a vision of the cross appeared to him at a battle at Milvian Bridge north of Rome, promising him victory under the sign of the cross. After his victory the use of the cross became widespread and from the fifth century on there are numerous examples in burial monuments, on royal urns, in the catacombs, and later on household utensils, medals, seals, and articles of devotion (Marucchi, 1908).

Contemporary cross with colored stones. 2" tall, $65–$85.

Early-1900s bronze crucifix with Matthew, Mark, Luke, and John images and symbols on ends of cross. 3" tall, $85–$95.

Late-1800s rose gold plated Jeanette cross, historically purchased by young maids in France with their first wages. 2" tall, $75–$95.

Two 1800s bronze reliquary crucifixes that can be opened to put the relic inside. 3"–4", $95–$125 each.

Early-1900s silver cross tied with ropes. 2" tall, $45–$55.

Early-1900s mother of pearl crucifix with stations of the cross, from Jerusalem. 11" tall, $135–$160.

Early-1900s brass cross with crown of thorns in center. 3" tall, $50–$60.

History of the Crucifixion and the Crucifix

On a hill called Golgotha (Calvary), outside the city of Jerusalem, three men were crucified. Scholars do not agree on the exact year. The years 30 AD and 33 AD have been suggested. At one time it was thought that the crucifixion took place on the thirteenth day of the Hebrew month of Nizan, the seventh month of the Hebrew calendar, which corresponds roughly from mid-March to mid-April, hence the tradition of the thirteenth being an unlucky day. One of the three men executed was called Jesus and His death and resurrection would change the world and the course of history.

The Hebrew word *golgotha* and its Latin translation, *calvary*, mean skull. The hill of Golgotha was desert-like and bare, with no vegetation, thus it was like a bald head or skull. Another possible origin of the name comes from the Jewish belief that the skull of Adam, the first man according to the Old Testament, was discovered there, where it had been buried. This is one of the possible explanations of the skull and cross bones at the foot of some crucifixes. Another explanation of these symbols is Christ's triumph over death. Christ rose from the dead and was resurrected. These symbols also represent the theme

Saint Benedict crucifix with ebony inlay. 3" tall, $50–$75.

1800s cast iron crucifix door knocker. 8" tall, $100–$125.

Early-1900s boxwood bead rosary with skull. 49" long, $95–$125.

Five 1800s rosary crucifixes with skull and crossbones at the bottom. $65–$75 each.

Early-1900s boxwood bead rosary with skulls reminding us that death is at hand. 65" long, $125–$150.

Early-1900s shepherd's cross with carved-bone Christ on three-tiered stand. This is known as a Jansenist cross as the arms are close together, indicating everlasting life for a chosen few. 12" tall, $100–$125.

of *memento mori*, from the Latin idea that translates as "remember that you must die"—a reminder to mankind that life is fragile and fleeting. Some of the older rosaries have a two-sided skull hanging from them and some have skulls strung among the beads. This skull or *caput mortem* (head of death) is unrelated to use of the skull by the Goth culture that is popular today. The skull motif is very prevalent in today's society in clothing, accessories, design, and decoration, usually without religious connotation. In John 19:17 there is a reference to the hill where Christ was crucified: "And he bearing his cross went forth into a place called the place of the skull, which is called in Hebrew Golgotha." In Mark 15:22 we read: "And they bring him into the Golgotha, which is, being interpreted, the place of a skull." The gospels of Matthew (27:33) and Luke (23:33) also make references to Golgotha and Calvary.

Early-1900s silver Holy Face of Jesus cross with symbols of Jesus. 2" tall, $55–$65.

Early-1900s mother of pearl Jerusalem crucifix with stations of the cross. 9" tall, $100–$125.

Early-1900s wood crucifix with porcelain holy font. 7" tall, $50–$65.

Seven early-1900s mother of pearl crosses and crucifixes, probably souvenirs from Jerusalem. 1½"–2½" tall, $40–$75 each.

Napoleon III orange velvet cross with filigree work. 14" tall, $125–$150.

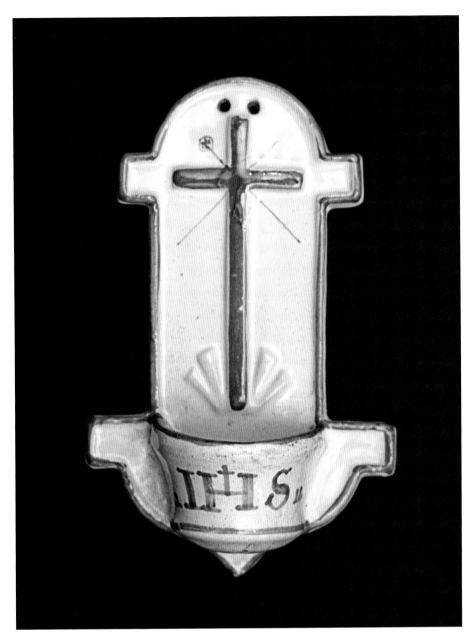

Early-1900s white faience holy font with blue cross and IHS initials of Jesus. 7" tall, $75 –$95.

Early-1900s silver Sacred Heart cross from Montmartre with medallion in center. Each end of the cross has the Chi Rho symbol and the symbols for Alpha and Omega are on each side of Christ. 1 ¾" tall, $75–$95.

The punishment and killing of Christ by nailing him to a cross represented a truculent and ignoble death. The word *crucifixion* comes from the Latin *crux*, cross, and the verb *figere*, to attach. Crucifixion as punishment for serious crimes was not commonly practiced by the Hebrews. Capital punishment for them was by stoning. However, when Palestine became part of the Roman Empire, this form of punishment was introduced. In Rome this form of punishment was used for criminal slaves. It was forbidden, however, to be used on Roman citizens.

The historical narrative of the Passion (Suffering) and Crucifixion of Jesus is told to us in the gospels of Matthew, Mark, Luke, and John in the New Testament. Jesus was punished for declaring himself king of the Jews, for this was considered treason against the Roman Emperor. In the gospel John 19:17-37, there is a description of the events leading up to the punishment of Jesus and his death on the cross, along with two criminals who suffered the same punishment. Pontius Pilate, the sixth Roman procurator of Judaea, placed a title over the head of Jesus on the cross: "And Pilate wrote a title, and put it on the cross."

Early-1900s shepherd's cross with carved-bone Christ on wood stand. Also known as a Jansenist cross. 13" tall, $100–$125.

Four late-1800s mother of pearl rosary crucifixes with silver ends. Approximately 3" tall, $100–$125 each.

Contemporary metal Jansenist crucifix. 6" tall, $40–$50.

Early-1900s brass crucifix with hidden knife. 3½" tall, $75–$95.

Napoleon III crimson velvet cross with elaborate crucifix and brass holy font at the base. 16" tall, $135–$175.

And the writing was, Jesus of Nazareth, The King of the Jews" (John 19:19). This is the origin of the letters INRI we see over the head of Christ on most crucifixes. These letters mean *Iesus Nazarenus Rex Iudaeorum*, Latin for Jesus of Nazareth King of the Jews. Some crucifixes have a nimbus over the head of Christ. This nimbus from the Latin word for cloud represents a radiance or light coming from the head of a holy person. The Bible describes in detail the death of Christ and his suffering on the cross.

There was a custom in these times of breaking the legs of those who died on the cross so they would die more quickly and could be removed from the cross in the evening. John 19:32–33 refers to this custom: "Then came the soldiers, and broke the legs of the first and of the other which was crucified with him. But when they came to Jesus and saw that he was dead already, they broke not his legs." Three days later Jesus arose from the dead and appeared to Mary Magdalene and his disciples (John: 20).

Napoleon III red velvet crucifix with holy water font at base. 10" tall, $75–$95.

Two silver contemporary crosses with skulls. 2" and 4" tall, $65–$75 each.

Early-1900s carved wood crucifix with porcelain holy water font at base. 9" tall, $75–$95.

Early-1900s cast iron frame shaped
like a cross. 12" tall, $75–$85.

Art deco Celtic oak cross with window
in center to place relic. 11" tall,
$125–$150.

Three early-1900s
elaborate German
filigree crosses. 2"–3"
tall, $75–$95 each.

Contemporary shell cross made into a pin. 2" tall, $20–$30.

Silver cross, dated 1902, with medallion showing the Virgin Mary and Christ in the center. Ends have fleur-de-lys design. 2" tall, $85–$95.

1900s shell crucifix. 10" tall, $65–$85.

The crucifix, a cross upon which the body of Christ was nailed, was not commonly used as a symbol of Christianity and a subject of art and embellishment until the sixth century. Over time the crucifix became the symbol of sacrifice and atonement for the sins of mankind. This symbol is a reminder of the love of Jesus and the hope of everlasting life. The crucifix is the symbol of Christianity used by practicing Catholics while most Protestants prefer the empty cross, choosing to focus on the message of Christ's resurrection rather than his suffering. Both can be seen as symbols of faith and hope. Both are displayed and worn to show devotion and reverence. Both the empty cross and the cross with the body of Christ represent the victory of Jesus over sin and death since he conquered death through his resurrection. Jesus sacrificed His life so that Christians could have everlasting life as promised in John 3:16.

Early-1900s silver First Communion cross. 2" tall, $75–$85.

Early-1900s white alabaster cross with painted flowers and Our Lady of Lourdes initials in center. 4" tall, $65–$85.

Contemporary metal cross showing Jesus on the cross and, in the background, Jesus risen from the dead. 2" tall, $20–$25.

1900s brass cross with thorn designs. 3" tall, $50–$60.

Three 1900s Celtic silver crosses. 1½"–2" tall, $45–$60 each.

Early-1900s bronze medal from the
Roman catacombs showing Chi Rho
symbol. 1" in diameter, $65–$75.

Early-1900s brass piece with engraved
cross in center. 9" in diameter, $75–$95.

1900s mosaic cross. 3" tall, $45–$55.

Two early-1900s jet crosses. 2" tall,
$60–$75 each.

Two 1800s Jerusalem crosses. The
small one is dated 1869. 1½"–2",
$75–$95 each.

Four early-1900s lockets with crosses.
½"–1" tall, $35–$45 each.

Napoleon III red velvet cross with
ornate crucifix and holy water font at
base. 14½" tall, $125–$150.

Early-1900s Caravaca cross
on red velvet with elaborate
tin frame. 10" × 12",
$150–$195.

Five late-1800s mother of pearl crucifixes.
Approximately 3" tall, $100–$125.

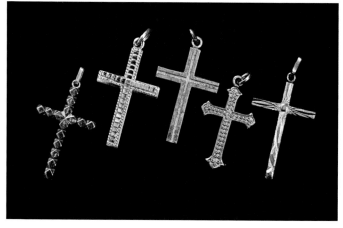

Five contemporary gold-plated crosses.
1"–1½", $25–$35 each.

The power of the cross comes from its symbolic meaning. Crosses have been used for centuries in both public and private devotion and are still popular today. There are crosses and crucifixes of all sizes with great variation in decoration and adornment. Sometimes they are very simple and nothing is added to the basic shape. They can be made from almost any material, from marble to plastic. People wear crosses as a sign of faith, often on a chain around the neck. Elaborate and expensive jewelry also often features the cross. This emblem of faith inspires an enormous amount of creative jewelry that is very popular today. Crosses seem to be everywhere. They are a very popular motif in tattoos as well as apparel and decoration. They are displayed in almost all churches, both Protestant and Catholic. We see crosses in cemeteries, on tombstones, country roads, on mountain tops, and in many public places. On the roadside we sometimes see simple wooden crosses that mark the place of an accident. Some people have religious shrines in their homes or crosses on the wall. In Europe as late as the nineteenth century there was a crucifix over the bed in almost every Catholic home. This powerful symbol of hope and protection is still strong in the third millennium.

Cross of Lorraine dated 1873 showing Sacred Heart and monogram of the Virgin Mary. 2" tall, $75–$85.

Three examples of equilateral crosses. $20–$85 each.

Early-1900s German silver filigree cross with pink stones. 4" tall, $100–$125.

Early-1900s silver Maltese cross with dove that represents the Holy Spirit. 2" tall, $65–$75.

Early-1900s brass Caravaca crucifix with angels. 2" tall, $45–$55.

Early-1900s amethyst cross with silver grape leaf ends. 2" tall, $95–$125.

Two early-1900s Lorraine crosses and filigree pin with Joan of Arc in the center surrounded by four gold Lorraine crosses. 1½"–2" tall, $50–$60 each.

Early-1900s elaborate rose gold plated
Maltese cross. 2" tall, $75–$95.

Early-1900s Bakelite cross with
angel. 7" tall, $85–$95.

Contemporary Yalalag silver cross from
Oaxaca, Mexico. 1¼" tall, $75–$100.

Art deco Bakelite cross with snake
curled around it. 3" tall, $45–$55.

Art deco Bakelite cross with ends shaped
like animal paws. 3" tall, $40–$50.

CHAPTER THREE
OBJECTS OF PERSONAL DEVOTION

Religious devotional artifacts have been displayed in the homes of both the rich and the poor for centuries. Most of the objects we will discuss in this chapter are from the 1800s and early 1900s. Many of these articles are available for collectors in shops, at antique fairs, and on the Internet. After World War II the production of these articles began to decline and one by one the small factories that produced these objects have closed or continued to operate in a very limited fashion with few artisans. Ambert, the "rosary making capital" of France at one time, no longer has factories making rosaries and the cottage industry of women making Rosaries at home has disappeared. There are Rosaries and other religious objects being made in Asia today but they can in no way compete with the craftsmanship and beauty of the older pieces and the materials used in their creation.

Articles of devotion are of a very personal nature and in the past, once they found their place in the home,

they stayed put. Often articles were buried with the faithful. At one time almost every Catholic home had several crucifixes, a small holy water font on the wall, a missal to take to Sunday Mass, and religious medals with images of Jesus, the Virgin Mary, or a favorite saint to be worn around the neck. Holy cards that commemorated special occasions were kept in the pages of the missal. Some of these objects are still used today, although not to the extent that they were in the past. The list of these objects is long so we will discuss only a selected number of these objects of personal piety that are remembrances of previous times.

In Protestant homes the Bible is the focus of devotion. At one time records of all family events were kept in the Holy Book. Reading the Bible is still an important family activity in many Protestant homes as well as some Catholic homes.

Early-1900s white bisque holy water font with Virgin Mary surrounded by flowers. 6" tall, $60–$75.

Small 1935 leather bound missal in original case. 3½" × 6", $75–$100.

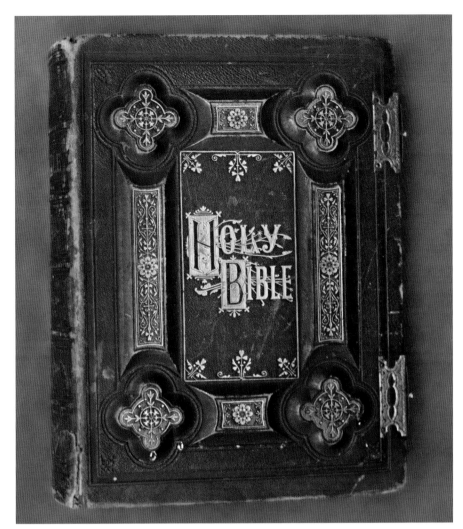

Napoleon III red velvet crucifix with holy water font at base. 10" tall, $75–$95.

1800s leather Holy Bible with metal clasps. 10½" × 14", $225–$275.

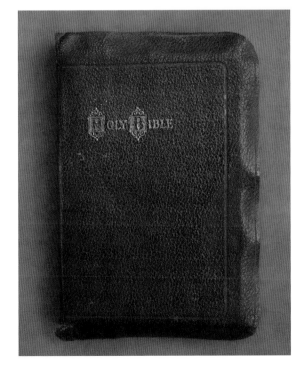

Well-worn leather family Holy Bible dated 1945, which belonged to the late Frank Knight. 6" × 9".

Pillow made from early-1900s ecclesiastical fragment with initials and crown of the Virgin Mary. 22" × 22", $600–$800. *Courtesy of Barbara Schooley.*

Early-1900s ex-voto enclosed in a silk heart and mounted on an anchor made of tiny shells. 6" × 8", $85–$125.

1939 Mexican retablo, Anastasio Correa gives thanks to the Virgin of Guadalupe for saving his life when he was a young soldier with Pancho Villa during the Mexican revolution. 11" × 7", $125–$150.

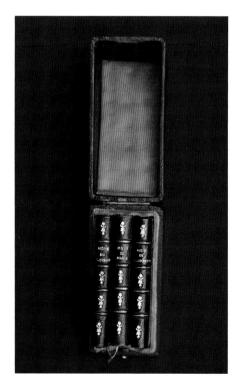

1800s set of three leather-bound religious books for months dedicated to Mary, Joseph, and the Sacred Heart in the original silk-lined box. 2" × 3", $350–$395 for the set.

Early-1900s Mexican retablo, A boy thanks Our Lady of San Juan de los Lagos for saving him from a wild dog. 11" × 9", $125–$150.

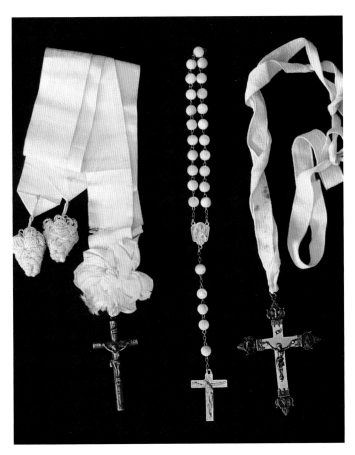

Three early-1900s First Communion crosses. $45–$85 each.

1800s ivory Book of Common Prayer in the original silk-lined box. 3" × 5", $250–$275.

Holy Water Fonts

Special containers for holy water have existed since ancient times. Catholic churches have large fonts at the entrance. Henri Leclerq explains the way holy fonts were used in early times: "Originally holy fonts in the churches were used by the faithful as part of a cleansing ritual. The faithful washed their hands and feet before entering the church itself" (Leclerq, 1910). In the Middle Ages there were separate fonts for different social classes. The clergy and the nobles had fonts reserved for them and only they could use this water. The poor, the bourgeoisie, and the working classes had to use a separate font. At Milhac-de-Nontron in the Dordogne region of France there was a special font for lepers.

The fonts used in homes are very small compared with those in churches. They have been reduced in size so that they will fit in a small space on a wall. They contain holy water from church fonts or chapels to be used by the family. Sometimes the water comes from a blessed spring that flows on the grounds outside a church or chapel and sometimes it comes from a Holy Water reservoir located in a church for the use of the faithful. Home fonts can be made of materials such as clay, porcelain, enamel, marble, pewter, copper, and alabaster, just to mention a few. They are made to be attached to a wall and have a small container for the water attached to the base of the artistic object. Extra water to replenish the fonts is often kept in special bottles for this purpose. These domestic holy fonts were immensely popular in the past but their production has tapered off since the end of World War I (Berthod, 2006, 41). They are placed near the bed, over the door, or over the sink and can even be built into the wall. Sometimes they were sold by traveling salesmen (colporteurs), as were many other religious articles.

Early-1900s wood cross with elaborate metal crucifix and holy water font at base. 7" tall, $65–$75.

Early-1900s Notre Dame de Lourdes souvenir wood plaque with glass holy water font. 6" tall, $35–$45.

Early-1900s glass holy water font with cross design. 6" tall, $60–$75.

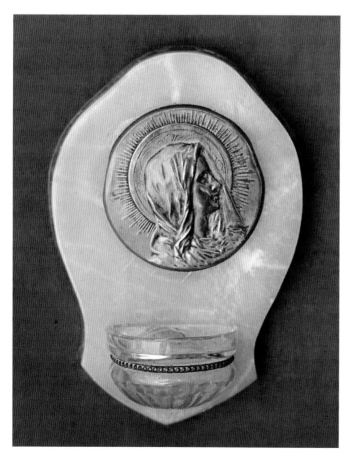

Early-1900s marble holy water font with brass medallion of the Virgin Mary. 5" tall, $75–$85.

Art deco wood plaque with bronze medallion of the Virgin Mary and glass holy water font. 5" tall, $30–$40.

Early-1900s wood crucifix with holy
water font at base. 12" tall, $60–$80.

Early-1900s mother of pearl holy water
font with portrait of the Virgin Mary
and Christ child. 5" tall, $85–$115.

Early-1900s bronze holy water font
with Virgin Mary. 11" tall, $100–$125.

Early-1900s porcelain holy water font with cross design and angel at the top. 7" tall, $75–$95.

Font-Sainte, a sacred fountain near Saint-Hippolyte in the Auvergne region of France, often visited by pilgrims.

Ex-votos

An ex-voto is an object offered to God, the Virgin, or a saint in return for a prayer or request answered. The term comes from Latin and is an abbreviated form of *ex voto suscepto*, or "from the vow made." Implicit in the concept of the ex-voto is the fact that the object will be displayed in a holy place such as a church altar or a prominent wall inside the church or chapel itself. Often accompanying the ex-voto will be a phrase such as "In gratitude for prayers answered." The ex-voto object has some kind of

relationship to the person who has received the favor. It also alludes to the request itself. It describes the miracle granted and personal information about the donor. It can also be a replica of a body part such as a leg, eyes, or arm, or an object belonging to the donor, or even his or her picture. This offering is pledged before the favor is granted.

Salvador Rodríguez Becerra, professor of cultural anthropology at the University of Seville, Spain, divides ex-votos into two groups. The first group is composed of narrative ex-votos such as pictures, letters, and documents: *el ex-voto pictórico*. The second group includes all other objects that are symbols of the vow made by the donor.

There have been a number of interesting recent studies done about the cultural and anthropological importance of the first group of ex-votos described by Rodríguez Becerra. The pictures and narratives offer important examples of what is called popular religion, that is, religious practices, beliefs, sentiments, and legends of humble people as opposed to more formal and traditional practices of the church. Rodríguez Becerra explains the importance of ex-votos as a rich cultural source. Besides their religious significance, ex-votos offer us a rare insight into the heart and mind of the faithful who are rarely heard from outside of their own personal world. (Rodríguez Becerra, 123–124) These examples of devotion can help us to understand the intimate surroundings of the creator and donor of the ex-voto. They offer us a narrative and often a picture of the accident, danger, or illness from which the victim or a family member was saved through divine intervention. In this case, the visual tells us everything.

Early-1900s group of metal ex-votos. $40–$50 each.

Three early-1900s Italian Sacred Heart ex-votos, two with initials for *per grazia ricevuta* (for grace received). 4" tall, $100–$150 each.

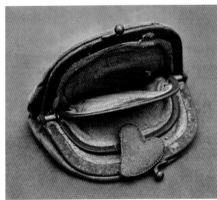

Early-1900s well-worn leather change purse with ex-voto inside. 1½" tall, $25–$35.

Early-1900s
group of small
ex-votos.
$20–$35 each.

Early-1900s
group of small
ex-votos.
$20–$35 each.

Early-1900s group of small ex-votos. $20–$35 each.

Contemporary group of Mexican ex-votos. $10–$15 each.

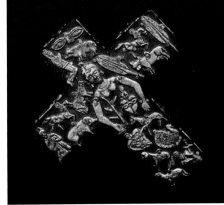

Contemporary Mexican wood cross covered with ex-votos. 6" tall, $75–$95.

Contemporary Mexican small wood shoe form covered with ex-votos. 6" long, $75–$95.

In the second group of ex-votos, a material object represents a symbol of the miracle performed. The list of these possible artifacts is endless. The object can be anything that represents a divine intervention or an answer to a prayer. Some examples would be replicas of body parts and human organs, a cross, a ship, metal replicas of domestic animals, a child's garment, a uniform from a soldier, a soccer jersey, a medal earned in battle, a wedding dress, and the list goes on. There could also be artifacts associated with a favorite saint such as the ox of Saint Luke, the lion of Saint Mark, or the roses of Saint Thérèse of Lisieux. In Cuba, Lina Ruz, the mother of Fidel and Raúl Castro, made a pilgrimage to the shrine of the patron saint of Cuba, the Virgin of Caridad del Cobre, asking her to protect her sons during the Sierra Maestra campaign against Batista. As an ex-voto, she left a small golden statue of a guerrilla soldier. Ernest Hemingway left his 1954 Nobel Prize at the shrine of the Virgin of Caridad, known affectionately as Cachita to the Cuban people, to show his gratitude for the award. The award was on display until 1986 when a visitor broke the display glass and stole it. Fortunately it was recovered a few days later but it is no longer on public display. Hernán Cortés, the Spanish conquistador, offered an ex-voto to the Virgin of Guadalupe of Extremadura, Spain, his native region. It was a gold scorpion decorated with forty emeralds and two pearls with the remains of the scorpion that had bitten him inside

Early-1900s Guatemalan coral and jet necklace with coins and ex-votos. 36" long, $225–$275.

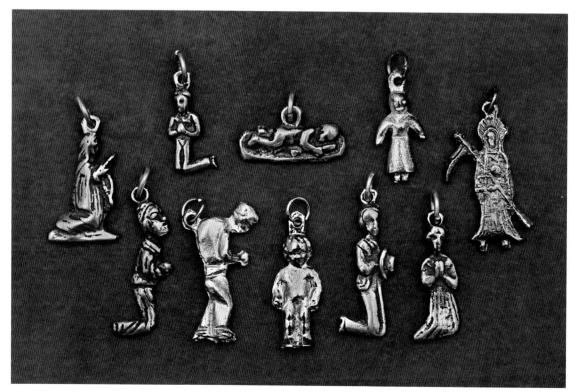

Contemporary Mexican silver ex-votos. $10–$15 each.

it (Durand, 1995, 2–3). He had prayed to her to save him from the scorpion's venom, and he survived.

Ex-votos give us a visual image of faith and gratitude and express very personal experiences with a divine being. They can be very informal, written in a very simple style with spelling mistakes and all, with no other goal than to give thanks for a miracle. María del Carmen Medina San Román, in her interesting article on votive art, explains that what ex-votos have in common "is that they were offered to a specific divinity, as a gesture of hope in the face of adversity or of gratitude for a favorable response by the divinity" (Medina San Román, 1997, 108).

1948 Mexican retablo, Two sisters thank Our Lady of San Juan de los Lagos for saving them when lightning struck a tree that fell on their house during a storm. 12" × 10", $125–$150.

1930s Mexican retablo, A fisherman gives thanks to the Virgin of Guadalupe for saving him when his boat overturned during a storm. 12" × 10", $125–$150.

1954 Mexican retablo, Enedino López gives thanks to the Virgin of Guadalupe for saving his life in the bullring. 11½" × 9½", $125–$150.

Estando en la feria de mi pueblo en san jose de grasia, la juana me reto a que le montara al toro y en ese momento me encomiende a la virgen de guadalupe que me ayude a salir de tan apurado trance. Enedino Lopez 1954.

1955 Mexican retablo, Ramiro Reyes gives thanks to the Virgin of Guadalupe for saving him when bandits attacked his bus and killed several of the passengers. 10½" × 6½", $125–$150.

VIAJANDO RUMBO AL PUERTO DE VERACRUZ POR EL CAMINO A PUEBLA SALIENDO DE LA CIUDAD DE MEXICO NOS ASALTARON UNOS FORAJIDOS MATANDO A VARIOS DE LOS VIAJEROS SALVANDOME YO AL ASERME EL MUERTO. POR ESOTE DOY LAS GRASIAS VIRGEN DE GUADALUPE. RAMIRO REYES. CIUDAD DE MEXICO 1955.

Reliquaries

Reliquaries are containers of the remains or partial relics of saints and holy people or vestiges of articles that belonged to them. They have existed since ancient Christian times. Their main purpose is to show the revered object, so their surfaces are transparent and often made of glass, allowing the faithful to see inside. An "authentic" relic has been sealed by a bishop who attests to its authenticity (Berthod, 2006, 236).

Reliquaries come in all sizes, from the size of a chestnut, made to fit into a pocket, to the large ones found in churches. Important relics are enclosed in glass cases in some churches. The reliquaries of most interest to our study are personal reliquaries found in private homes and used by individuals to protect them from harm. Sometimes they are worn around the neck or even sewn inside clothing. Others are carried in the pocket as a testimony to faith and a desire for protection (Berthod, 2006, 236).

Reliquaries were sometimes made by nuns in convents and are veritable works of art. These reliquaries can be found in museums and private collections.

Individuals also made intricate reliquaries with tiny images and bands of paper that explain the relic. The objects in the reliquary can be symbolic or realistic, showing a religious experience or devotion. The detail on these small works of art is noteworthy. The calligraphy is an art in itself.

Late-1800s oval framed reliquary of the Virgin of Carmel. 4" × 3", $95–$125.

1800s oval framed reliquary with intricate gilded paper designs surrounding the frame. 4" × 3", $75–$85.

Early-1900s Saint Thérèse reliquary with her picture and fragments of her clothing. $50–$60.

Late-1800s Mexican reliquary with the Virgin of the Rosary on one side and the Virgin of Guadalupe on the other. 2½" in diameter, $95–$145.

1800s framed decorated reliquary with the Virgin of Carmel and Saint Thérèse and Saint Claire in the center. 4½" × 6", $150–$175.

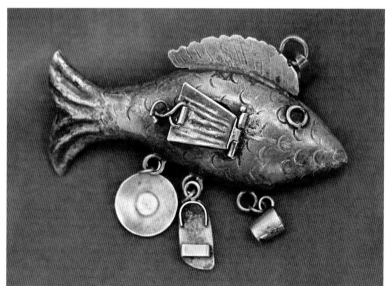

Early-1900s Guatemalan silver fish reliquary with small silver ex-votos. 3" long, $125–$150.

1800s reliquary of Saint Mary of the Angels. 3" in diameter, $125–$145.

Religious Textiles

Religious banners are used in processions and can also be seen in churches. They are beautifully decorated on satin or silk, sometimes hand painted or embroidered with intricate gold or silver thread. Sometimes they are adorned with beaded ornamentation. The banner may have the image of the patron saint, holy person, or the name of the religious brotherhood that sponsors the event. The banner is attached to a pole and is displayed in the procession. Later it is returned to the church and put on display.

Cotton textiles with religious themes are not common. However in the toiles of the late eighteenth and nineteenth centuries we occasionally see religious scenes or stories from the Bible. Many engravers of the early toiles (popular printed cottons) were Protestant workers, descendants of textile workers who had fled from France after the revocation of the Edict of Nantes that had granted them religious

freedom. The Edict of Versailles of 1788, also known as the Edict of Tolerance, once again offered freedom of religion to Protestants and restored their civil rights. Textile workers who later returned to work in the booming cotton print industry were careful to avoid religious controversy and thus avoided religious themes.

Ecclesiastic vestments are a rich source of valuable textiles of the past. They are adorned with gold and silver *passementerie* (elaborate trims) and exquisite embroidery and silks. Unfortunately these fragile items have suffered over the years, especially when stored in humid areas where they are often attacked by insects and rats. Some of the vestments have been discarded, burned, or sold at auction to be used in decoration. The emblems and trims are removed and made into pillows and other decorative articles, especially when the vestments are in very poor

Detail of early-1900s Sacred Heart banner with stumpwork (raised embroidery) gold letters and flowers and couching in the center crown of thorns. 21" × 37", $650–$800.

Black velvet stole with silver stumpwork, metallic tassels, and fringe, decorated on both sides. $250–$275.

Detail of early-1900s silver altar piece with Saint Roch and Saint Rose stumpwork letters and long silver fringe. $700–$800.

1700s fragment embroidered with metallic thread from a religious piece. 10" in diameter, $195–$250.

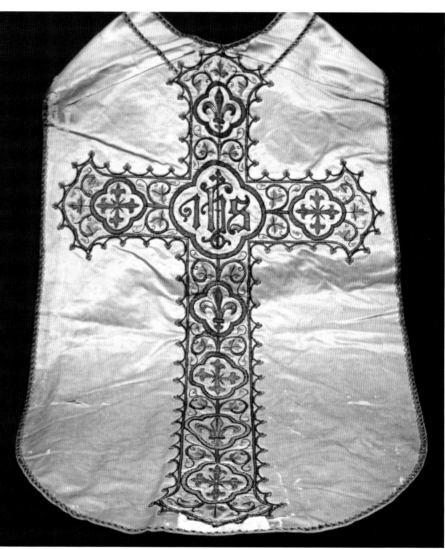

Early-1900s chasuble with IHS (Jesus) in the center and gold stumpwork. $350–$450.

Detail of aqua silk moiré altar piece with
hand-beaded crosses with fleur-de-lys ends
and silver metallic lace trim. $350–$400.

Early-1900s silver metallic altar piece
detail with monogram of the Virgin
Mary and flowers in stumpwork and
long silver fringe. $650–$750.

1700s silk embroidered fragment from
religious piece. 14" in diameter,
$195–$225.

condition. Silk is extremely delicate and cannot survive
light or dampness and will rip apart when handled.

The very best examples of this art are in museums,
but individual collectors frame them and hang them on
their walls or mantelpieces in their homes. The workmanship
on these sacred textiles is exquisite. The tendency today

in ecclesiastic robes is one of much greater simplicity and
economy of materials and decoration. However, there is
a movement toward more elaborate vestments and religious
articles in general. For a while they were difficult to find,
but now most liturgical supply houses carry a line of
traditional and less modern items.

Two fragments from a religious banner dated 1862 with metallic stumpwork and couching. $150–$175 for the pair.

Pair of 1860s figures from a religious banner with couching and stumpwork. 9" in diameter, $250–$300 a pair.

Two 1600s religious fragments with gold metallic and silk embroidered figures. 7" and 14", $250–$275 for the pair.

Detail of early-1900s American altar piece with gold sequin crosses. $150–$175.

Early-1900s fragment from a religious banner, representing the Virgin Mary with her foot on a serpent (conquering evil). 24" tall, $250–$300.

Early-1900s silk chasuble with IHS (Jesus) in the center and elaborate gold stumpwork. $400–$500.

Detail of early-1900s chasuble with *Agnus Dei* (Lamb of God) motif in the center with elaborate gold stumpwork. $550–$650.

Early-1900s satin church piece with Virgin Mary and Christ child in the center and intricate silk embroidery and couching. 23" × 23", $550–$650.

Missals and Religious Books

The term *missal* comes from the Latin *missale*, from *missa*, Mass. It is a book of prayers said by the priest at the altar and also contains everything that is read or sung in connection with the offering of the Holy Sacrifice during the ecclesiastical year (Thurston, 1911). They are often translated from Latin into the modern languages. The missals studied and illustrated in this book are the Roman missals, so called because they are used in Catholic churches where the Latin rite is used. These missals have two parts. The first part contains the part of the liturgy that is said at every Mass and the second part is dedicated to parts of the liturgy that vary according to special feasts and seasons (Thurston, 1911).

There are two kinds of missals. Altar missals, used by the presiding priest, are usually large. The second kind is much smaller and is for personal use. For a complete explanation of the development and history of the missal, see Herbert Thurston's article on the missal in *The Catholic Encyclopedia*. We will focus on personal missals as well as show other religious books.

In addition to the importance of the missal as a book of prayers, the beauty and elaborate workmanship of these books is notable. Some are made of ivory; others are hand-tooled leather with ornamental clasps. The paper of the beautiful pages is of the very best quality and is sometimes

Pair of red leather–bound books dated 1879 with gold pages. 3½" × 5", $250–$300 for the pair.

Set of four leather-bound missals—the four seasons, dated 1891, in original box. 2¾" × 4", $375–$400 for the set.

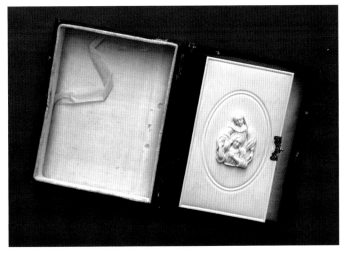

1800s ivory missal with Virgin and Christ child on the cover, silver clasp and blue velvet spine, in original silk moiré box. 4" × 5", $300–$350.

Set of four leather-bound missals—the four seasons, dated 1902, in original box. 3" × 4", $425–$475 for the set.

edged in 24-carat gold. They were often presented as gifts for special occasions such as marriage or First Communion. There are more simple ones that are also well made, usually in leather or pigskin. Some of them were never used and are still in the original boxes. Others are well worn from use and devotion. Missals are small and could be carried comfortably in a pocket or purse. In France, there were editorial houses in Lyons, Limoges, and Tours just to mention a few, that dedicated their business to producing and selling missals. They also printed missals for other countries, like Spain. As evidenced by the number of beautiful missals on the market today, these volumes were treasured and carefully preserved. Our illustrations show a wide selection of these French missals and religious books.

Three 1800s leather-bound missals with elaborate clasps. Approximately 3½" × 5½", $125-$150 each.

Two 1800s leather-bound missals with elaborate silver clasps. 3½" × 4½", $150–$175 each.

Two 1800s missals with elaborate silver clasps; one dated 1859, the other 1867. 3½" × 4½", $150–$175 each.

Three early-1900s religious leather-bound books. 3½" × 6", $295–$350 for the set.

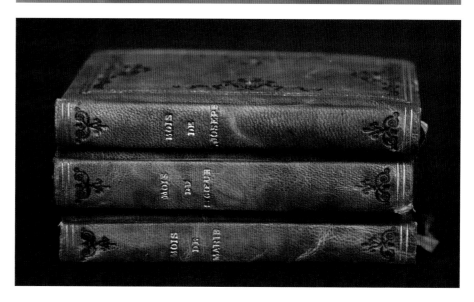

1888 leather-bound missal with IHS in gold on the front. 3" × 4", $100–$125.

Reverse side of the previous book, showing the initial of the Virgin Mary with a crown.

Pair of 1879 religious books with green leather and green pages, owned by Sixte O'Gorman. 3" × 4¾", $250–$275 for the pair.

The same book, showing the green interior pages.

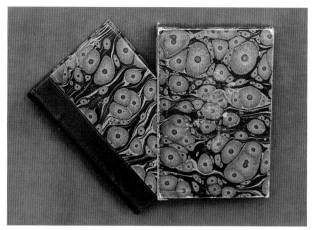

1891 religious book with marbled paper cover and leather binding in original matching box. 3" × 4¾", $100–$125.

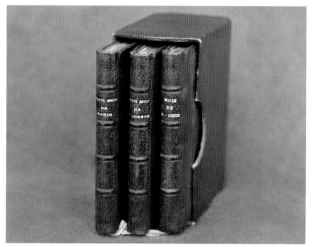

1933 leather-bound missal with gold pages. 3" × 4¾", $75–$95.

Set of three 1800s leather-bound religious books in original box. 3" × 4½", $250–$275 for the set.

Group of 1800s miniature leather-bound books. Approximately 3" × 4", $100–$125 each.

Commemorative Objects

There are many artifacts that serve as mementoes of important personal events that mark the high points of religious life for Catholics. The first event is baptism, a happy occasion where the baby is surrounded by family and friends in a special Mass. In France, pink, blue, or white almonds are stored in special boxes and given to the guests. Other gifts for the child include tiny gold pins with a religious medal or a little gold ring with the image of the Virgin. For the nursery there may be a cradle cross with an angel or a special marble and bronze plaque with a guardian angel, a dove that represents the Holy Spirit, or the Virgin—or a combination of these motifs. These are hung on the wall by the baby's cradle.

Almond box for the baptism of a little girl.

Baptism invitation. $6–$7.

Early-1900s white marble cradle cross with angel in center. 6" tall, $225–$275.

Box for almonds, traditionally given in France to guests at a baptism. This box is for the baptism of a little boy. $10–$15.

Art deco Bakelite cradle plaque with silver medallion of the Virgin Mary. 2½" tall, $35–$45.

Three early-1900s marble cradle plaques, each with a dove (Holy Spirit). 4½"–5½". $125–$150 each.

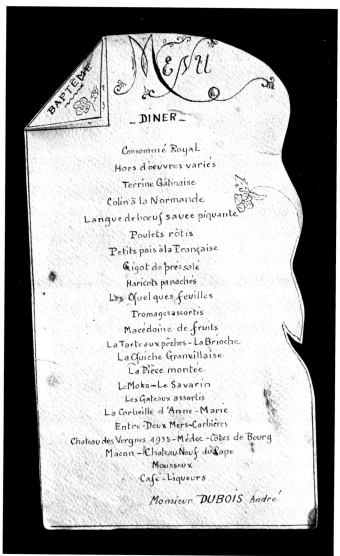

1947 menu for a baptism dinner. $18–$25.

First Communion is of great importance and is celebrated by all Catholic families usually before the child reaches the age of twelve. The future communicants prepare for this event together and celebrate a special Mass all at the same time. Often, guests are invited afterward to private family celebrations. The girls wear white dresses and veils and, depending on the country, the boys also wear white or are dressed in their best clothes. There are many souvenirs of the First Communion such as holy cards showing scenes of the Eucharist. The older cards are quite elaborate with names engraved in gold. An important gift for the occasion may be a mother of pearl rosary, a very special one to be kept and treasured always. There may also be a beautiful missal with a name engraved on it, or a tiny mother of pearl change purse or a little satin purse

to carry during the ceremony. There are also silver medals given for First Communion. Many of these are engraved with a name and date.

The next important occasion is the marriage ceremony. Keepsakes include the bride's lace veil, wax orange blossoms made into a crown to decorate the veil, a special mother of pearl rosary, a leather-bound or ivory missal, even satin wedding slippers. There may be a very special cross or religious medal given to the bride to be worn during the wedding service.

Sometimes these souvenirs are preserved in a special arrangement under a small glass dome. Many of these objects are handed down in families from one generation to the other. Hand-written menus from a special luncheon or dinner are also saved as a souvenir.

Early-1900s First Communion pillow.
7" × 7", $25–$35.

Early-1900s First Communion picture.
$5–$10.

Early-1900s tin framed First
Communion picture. 3¾" × 5", $40–$50.

Four early-1900s First Communion
pictures. $5–$10 each.

Early-1900s boy's moiré arm band and
commemorative holy card. $35–$45.

Three early-1900s First Communion figures. 8"–10" tall, $40–$50 each.

Three early-1900s First Communion purses with embroidery and lace. $25–$35 each.

Early-1900s First Communion figure in a wood box. 5½" tall, $45–$55.

Three early-1900s First Communion bisque figures. 3"–4" tall, $20–$30 each.

1930 menu for First Communion ceremony. $15–$20.

First Communion picture of Philippe Laval, priceless.

Early-1900s marble plaque commemorating First Communion. 3" in diameter, $35–$45.

Early-1900s ivory change purse, souvenir of First Communion. 2" tall, $50–$65.

Early-1900s metal plaque commemorating First Communion, 6" in diameter, $50–$60.

1947 wedding invitation and
dinner menu. $18–$20.

Early-1900s silver First
Communion medal. $65–$85.

Art nouveau silver First
Communion medal. $65–$85.

The Mustard Seed

Difficult times in life are also symbolized by devotional
objects. One inspiring example is that of the mustard seed.
The symbol of the mustard seed has long been associated
with religion. The Bible mentions the strength of faith and
relates it to the mustard seed. In Matthew 13:31–32 we
read: "The kingdom of heaven is like to a grain of mustard
seed which a man took and sowed in his field/Which
indeed is the least of all seeds: but when it is grown, it is
the greatest among herbs, and becometh a tree, so that
the birds of the air come and lodge in the branches thereof."

The mustard seed in this parable is a symbol of the
Church, which grew from a small seed into a flourishing
and powerful institution much like a tree that starts from a
small seed. This symbol is also used for inspiration for those
with serious health problems, especially women. As a sign
of faith and hope they wear a tiny mustard seed encased in
glass around their neck or on a pin. These mustard seeds
made into jewelry were very popular in the 1940s and 1950s
and are making a comeback today. Another passage in the
Bible in Luke 17:6 tells us: "And the Lord said: If you had
faith as a grain of mustard seed, ye might say unto the
sycamine tree, Be thou plucked up by the root, and be thy
planted in the sea; and it would obey you."

Four small mustard seeds globes popular in the United
States in the 1940s and 1950s. $25–$35 each.

Three mustard seeds globes popular in the United States in
the 1940s and 1950s. $25–$35 each.

Paper Ephemera: Holy Cards

Catholic holy cards represent a tradition. These little treasures were often given as souvenirs of important events such as baptism, First Communion, weddings, pilgrimages, and funerals. They were usually dated and carried the name of the person celebrated. We find them tucked away in drawers, and used as bookmarks in Bibles, books, and missals. They were also collected and saved either as a collection or as a remembrance of a special event. Many of the holy cards have pictures of popular saints such as Saint Thérèse of Lisieux, Saint Anthony, Saint Joseph, and also of Jesus, the Virgin Mary, and the Eucharist. Some are quite elaborate with beautiful engraving, muted colors, and elaborate gold borders.

Most of the elaborate and artistic holy cards, especially those with wide lace borders, are in private collections. However, there are many beautiful holy cards still available on the market today if one wants to assemble a collection. For those interested in holy card treasures, there are publications, websites and collector groups on the subject.

Four early-1900s First Communion holy cards. $6–$7.

Five early-1900s First Communion holy cards. $6–$7.

CHAPTER FOUR
THE SAINTS

The first saints were martyrs who died for their Christian faith. Stephen, the first martyr, was stoned to death by the Jews because he proclaimed that Jesus was the Messiah announced in the Scriptures. The first saints and those who came later lived a life of faith and piety often sacrificing their lives for their beliefs. These men and women did not become saints based on their faith alone. They also lived exemplary lives and spent their time on Earth actively engaged in doing good works for others, especially those in need. Most saints are associated with specific regions, causes, professions, and events and have special symbols associated with them. These saints are called patron saints and are invoked for guidance in times of need. For example, Saint Jude and Saint Rita are called upon for desperate causes and problems.

In 1969 changes were made to simplify the official liturgical calendar with the reforms of the Second Vatican Council. For example, after changes to the calendar, the archangels Michael, Gabriel, and Raphael are celebrated on the same day: September 29. Some saints were eliminated from the calendar but that does not mean that they were officially "decanonized." Thus not all saints are listed in the official liturgical calendar. Dates of celebration of a feast day usually refer to the death of the saint.

Two early-1900s brooches with images of the apparition of the Virgin Mary at Lourdes. 1"–2", $35–$45 each.

Early-1900s framed picture of Saint Anthony. 3" × 5", $85–$95.

Bronze medal of Saint Catherine of Siena. $35–$45.

Reverse side of the medal in the previous picture.

Framed collection of early-1900s silver religious medals. $250–300.

Five early-1900s brooches with image of Joan of Arc. $45–$55 each.

Four 1900s steel dies used to stamp religious medals. $25–$50 each.

Three 1900s steel dies used to stamp religious medals. $25–$50 each.

Early-1900s Benedictine cross named for Saint Benedict. Symbols of the saint are behind the head of Christ. 2½" tall, $50–$60.

Four 1900s steel dies used to stamp religious medals. $25–$50 each.

Since the beginning of Christianity people have told stories about the lives of saints. Over the centuries, these stories became embellished, sometimes entering the realm of legend. How many saints are there? The official lists of saints published over the centuries have enumerated thousands. The study of the lives of saints is known as hagiography, from the Greek *hagio*, which means saint. Often these biographies of saints were idealized and exaggerated. The *Bibliotheco Sanctorum* had over eighteen volumes as of 1989 and lists over 10,000 saints. More than four hundred of those listed have been canonized by the popes (Woodward, 1990, 51). To "canonize" refers to official approval of the Roman Catholic Church and means that after an exemplary person dies, after a lengthy deliberation he or she is officially declared by the pope to be worthy of universal public veneration. There must also be documentation of a miracle associated with the person being considered for sainthood.

Early-1900s holy card depicting Saint Roch. $6–$7.

1900s metal statue of Saint Michael slaying a dragon (the devil). 3" tall, $40–$50.

Two early-1900s boxes showing Saint Bernadette. $30–$40 each.

1900s silver medal of Saint Patrick, $45–$50.

Our study of saints will be limited to a brief history of a few of the more popular saints. Every day of the year corresponds to one or more saints and that day is celebrated in honor of the saint. Sometimes that day is a local or national holiday in certain countries. At one time it was customary to name a child for the saint whose feast day corresponded to the day of the birth of the child. The fascination with the saints reached its peak in the Middle Ages but is still a subject of great interest and popularity today even among non-Catholics. Their stories and history are so powerful that even though their historical existence cannot be verified, their legends live on through popular devotion. What follows is an introductory study of some of the most inspirational and beloved saints. Stories of the lives of the saints vary greatly in the biographies and dictionaries of saints and often there is a mixture of history and legend in their stories.

Necklace made from religious medals and broken rosary beads. 27" long, $175–$195.

Necklace made from religious medals and broken rosary beads with large medallion of Joan of Arc. 29" long, $175–$195.

Bracelet made from antique buckle and religious medals. $100–$125.

Saint Andrew (November 30): Patron Saint of Fishermen (First Century)

Brother of Saint Peter, Saint Andrew was a fisherman at Capharnium (Galilee). He was one of the first to follow Jesus. From the tenth century on, he is represented by a cross in the form of an X, the type of cross used in his crucifixion. He is tied to the cross by ropes. Sometimes he has the symbol of a net filled with fish. He is invoked against injustice, sterility, gout, and dysentery and is the patron saint of Scotland, Burgundy (France), and Santander (Spain).

Early-1900s colored lithograph of Saint Andrew with x-shaped cross in the background, called a Saint Andrew cross. 7" × 10", $20–$30.

SAINT ANDRÉ

Saint Anne (July 26): Patron Saint of Grandmothers, Seamstresses, and Lace Makers (First Century)

Saint Anne was the mother of the Virgin Mary and grandmother of Jesus. Her name means "grace." According to tradition, Anne and her husband Joachim had waited twenty years for a child. Finally an angel appeared to them to announce the birth of a daughter, Mary. Anne was first honored in Jerusalem in the sixth century. Her fame reached its zenith in the fourteenth and fifteenth centuries and was especially venerated by the Franciscans and the Carmelites. She was also very popular during the Middle Ages in Spain where they called her *abuelita*, or little grandmother (Ladame, 1985, 121). In the seventeenth century she became very popular in Brittany where a basilica was built in her honor at Auray. Saint Anne was declared the patron saint of Brittany by Pope Pius X.

Two 1900s HR Quimper statues of Saint Anne. The left is 3½", $75–$95 and the right is 9", $145–$195.

1900s HR Quimper statue of Saint Anne and the young Virgin Mary. 9" tall, $175–$225.

1900s holy card of Saint Anne d'Auray, patron saint of Britany. $6–$7.

1900s framed picture of Saint Anne d'Auray under convex glass. 4½" × 5½", $85–$115.

Saint Anthony of Padua (June 13): Patron Saint of Lost Objects (1195–1231)

Saint Anthony was born in Portugal and died in Padua, Italy. He was one of the most learned and revered preachers of his time and traveled all over Europe having great spiritual success. He was canonized only one year after his death. He was a healer and was able to grant impossible favors. His special gift of recovering lost items stems from an episode in his life when he recovered a book stolen from his room by a monk who was embarking on a journey. Saint Anthony prayed for the return of his book, and the thief brought back the cherished book. Since then we call on Saint Anthony to help us recover lost articles, reciting: "Saint Anthony, Saint Anthony, please come around. Something's been lost and can't be found!" He is often portrayed with a book in his hands.

Two early-1900s holy cards showing Saint Anthony. $6–$7 each.

Early-1900s brass plaque with silver medallion of Saint Anthony of Padua. 5" × 6", $95–$125.

Early-1900s silver rosary case with image of Saint Anthony and rosary inside. 1½" in diameter, $45–$55.

Two early-1900s medals of Saint Anthony. $35–$45.

Two early-1900s medallions of Saint Anthony. $45–$50 each.

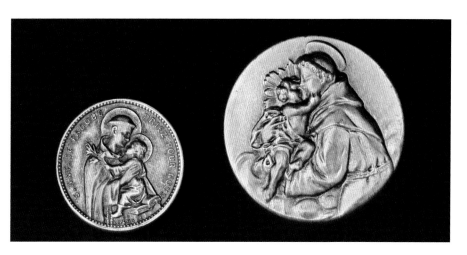

Saint Benedict of Nursia (July 11): Patron Saint of Monks, Farmers, and Chemists (480–550 ?)

Saint Benedict was born in Nursia, Italy. At the age of twenty, he became a hermit and lived several years in a grotto. In 529 he founded the great abbey of Monte Cassino, where he formulated the Benedictine rules. His motto was "Pray and work." His twin sister, Sister Scholastica, became a nun and was later canonized. The religious medal of Saint Benedict is one of the most popular medals worn today. The faithful wear the medal for protection from evil, sickness, and accidents. On the front of the medal is the image of Saint Benedict with his three symbols: the book, the cross, and the crow. The Latin inscriptions on the reverse side of the medal invoke the help of Benedict to ward off temptation and evil. We read the letters CSPB, which are Latin abbreviations for *Crux Sancti Patris*

Benedicti, meaning Cross of Holy Father Benedict. In the middle of the cross are the Latin letters CSSML, which stand for *Crux Sacra Sit Mihi Lux* or Holy Cross Be My Light. Finally we see the letters ND on the left and MD on the right, which stand for *Non Draco Sit Mihi Dux* or No Dragon, Do Not Be My Guide. On the outside circle of the medal, proceeding clockwise are the letters VRS, abbreviations for *Vade Retro Satan* meaning: Go Away, Retreat, Satan. Next is NSMV or *Nunquam Suade Mihi Vana*, which means No, You Will Never Persuade Me to Follow Your Foolishness. The next initials are SMQL for *Sunt Mala Quoe Libas*, or You Deliver Evil. Finally we see IVB for *Ipse Venena Bibas*, which we translate as, Keep Your Poison and Drink It Yourself.

Five early-1900s Saint Benedict medals. $35–$50 each.

Three early-1900s Saint Benedict medals. $35–$45 each.

Four early-1900s Saint Benedict medals. $35–$50 each.

Two early-1900s Saint Benedict medals. $40–$50 each.

Reverse side of the medals in the above picture, showing symbols of Saint Benedict.

Reverse side of the medals in the above picture.

Saint Bernadette (April 16): Patron Saint of Serious Illnesses (1844–1879)

One of six children, this shepherdess from a poor family saw the Virgin Mary eighteen times in 1858 in Lourdes, in southwestern France. It was not until the sixteenth vision that the Virgin revealed her identity saying: "I am the Immaculate Conception." Mary led her to a hidden spring that had healing powers. Bernadette decided later to enter the order of the Sisters of Charity. The site at Lourdes has become one of the major pilgrimage destinations in the world, attracting at least four million visitors a year who come to be healed of their illnesses.

Two early-1900s Saint Bernadette medals. $40–$50 each.

Early-1900s porcelain image of the apparition of the Virgin Mary to Saint Bernadette at Lourdes in elaborate brass frame with holy water font at base. 3" × 4". $135–$150.

Early-1900s hand-painted brooch framed in gold representing the apparition of the Virgin Mary to Saint Bernadette at Lourdes. 1½" × 2", $95–$125.

Early-1900s colored lithograph of the apparition of the Virgin Mary to Saint Bernadette at Lourdes. $20–$25.

Saint Catherine Labouré and the Miraculous Medal (November 28): Patron Saint of the Sick and the Poor (1806–1876)

Saint Catherine entered the order of the Sisters of Charity and shortly after her entrance in 1830, she received several apparitions of Mary Immaculate, which led to the creation of the Miraculous Medal. The Virgin Mary appeared to Catherine in her convent on Rue du Bac in Paris asking to have a medal struck in her honor, which would be oval in shape and have the following words:" O Mary conceived without sin, pray for us who have recourse to Thee." Mary promised that all who wore the medal would be blessed, receive graces, and receive the protection of God. The medal had appeared as a sort of oval frame about the Virgin's face. Suddenly, this oval frame turned around and on the other side appeared the initial "M" mounted on a cross, and under the name of Mary there were the Holy

Hearts of Jesus and His Mother. The first heart had a crown of thorns and the second one was pierced by a sword. Catherine told her spiritual director Father Aladel about the apparitions but kept them a secret from everyone else for her entire life. Because of this, she is often called the Saint of Silence. The medal was struck and almost immediately miracles began to happen to some who wore them. At first the medal was called the Medal of the Immaculate Conception, but it quickly became known as the Miraculous Medal because of the enormous number of miracles, cures, and acts of protection credited to it. According to the Association of the Miraculous Medal, by the time of Saint Catherine's death, over a billion medals had been distributed in the world.

Two early-1900s Miraculous Medals. $60–$70 each.

Reverse side of the medals in the previous picture, showing the monogram of the Virgin Mary.

Two early-1900s Miraculous Medals. $60–$70 each.

Reverse side of the medals in the previous picture, showing the monogram of the Virgin Mary.

Saint Cecilia (November 22): Patron Saint of Musicians, Poets, and Singers (Died circa 230))

Saint Cecilia is one of the most popular of the Roman martyrs. She was a young Christian who was engaged to be married but refused to give up her vow of chastity. She was married anyway and was able to convert her husband Valerian to Christianity, and he also died a martyr. Cecilia was decapitated for refusing to give sacrifice to the Roman gods. She is associated with music because during her wedding ceremony she refused to sing, saying that she would only sing to God. From the fifth century on she is shown with musical instruments, especially the organ and the lute.

Early-1900s holy card with Saint Cecilia. $6–$7.

Three early-1900s medals of Saint Cecilia. $45–$55 each.

Saint Christopher (July 25): Patron Saint of Travelers (Third Century)

We have no historical knowledge of Saint Christopher's life. According to legend, Saint Christopher was born in the third century. His name means bearer of Christ. He was a Christian from Asia Minor who served in the Roman armies and died a martyr for refusing to deny his faith. He was a giant figure who lived by a river with no bridge. Christopher helped travelers cross the river by carrying them on his huge shoulders. One day he transported a child who became extremely heavy as they crossed the river. Christopher was only able to reach the other side by using extreme effort and all the strength he could muster. The child was Jesus; he was so heavy because he bore the burden of mankind. Saint Christopher is always portrayed with a child on his shoulder. Since his historical existence could not be verified, he was removed from the liturgical calendar in 1970. However the people refuse to let go of him and he is still venerated today.

Early-1900s Saint Christopher images. $35–$60.

Early-1900s Saint Christopher medals. $35–$45.

Early-1900s Saint Christopher medals. $35–$45.

Early-1900s Saint Christopher bronze medallion that says, "Look at Saint Christopher then go on your way, reassured," signed by the engraver. 8" in diameter, $75–$85.

Saint Dominic (August 8): Patron Saint of Television Broadcasters, Orators, Communications Workers, and Astronomers (1171–1221)

Two early-1900s Saint Dominic medals. $45–$55.

Born in 1171 in the Castile region of Spain into the illustrious Guzmán family, Saint Dominic studied at the University of Palencia. In 1206 he went as a missionary to Languedoc (France) to combat the Albigensian heresy. He founded the Dominican order in 1216. According to tradition, the Virgin Mary appeared to Dominic in Albi, France, and gave him a rosary. It is because of his devotion to the rosary that the Albigensian heresy was defeated, and he thus is associated with the rosary. He is sometimes portrayed with a dog at his feet, with a torch in the dog's mouth. This alludes to a dream his mother had before he was born in which this image of the dog appeared. The animal is the dog of the Lord: *Domini canis.* Thus the dog became the symbol of the Dominican order, the watchdogs of the Lord. Saint Dominic was known for his powerful sermons, and it is said that he set the world on fire with his preaching. He is the patron saint of astronomers because of his dedication to scholarship and the patron saint of orators because of his preaching of the goodness of God's creation.

Saint Francis of Assisi (October 4): Patron Saint of Animals and Nature (1182(?)–1226)

Saint Francis was born around 1182 in Italy. After a misspent youth he entered the service of God. For two years he lived as a hermit. He tried to imitate Christ in his life. By 1208 Francis had a calling to live in absolute poverty while preaching the word of God. His reputation for sacrifice and poverty earned him the name of *Poverello*, which means "the poor one." There are many legends concerning his life. He loved nature, plants, and animals. Francis preached sermons to the birds and according to a famous story tamed a wolf near the town of Gubbio. He wrote Canticle of the Sun, a prayer in thanks of God's creation. Many parishes have an animal blessing on October 4 on the feast day of Saint Francis. He founded the Franciscan order and preached throughout Italy, Spain, and Egypt. Upon his return to Italy he once again took up his life as a hermit, and in 1224 he began to receive the stigmata from the wounds of Christ. He became blind; his health declined, and he died in 1226. Some of his contemporaries thought he was Christ returned to the world.

Early-1900s Saint Francis of Assisi holy card. $6–$7.

Saint George (April 23): Patron Saint of England, Arms, and the Cavalry (Died circa 303)

Saint George was a popular saint from Palestine. His deeds are legendary, such as his role as a heroic soldier in the Imperial army and his bravery in slaying the dragon that was terrorizing Libya. According to tradition, he was a noble who suffered a seven-year martyrdom of torture and pain before his death. After the first crusade, Saint George became the patron of the knights of the Crusades, especially the Templars, whose order was founded in 1118. The equestrian figure of this saint killing a dragon is common in sacred art.

Early-1900s Saint George medals, $35–$50.

Early-1900s framed bronze image of Saint George. 8" × 8½", $100–$125.

Early-1900s Saint George medals. $35–$50.

Early-1900s Saint George holy card. $6–$7.

Saint James (July 25): Patron Saint of Spain and Guatemala, Pharmacists, and Pilgrims (Died circa 44)

Saint James was one of the twelve apostles. He was the first apostle to be martyred for Christianity under Herod Agrippa (37–44). According to tradition, his remains were found in Compostela, in the region of Galicia, Spain, in the ninth century. He was first portrayed in art as a pilgrim, but after the battle of Clavijo in the year 844, he usually appeared on a white horse fighting the Maures. His tomb in what is now called Santiago de Compostela has been a major pilgrimage destination since the Middle Ages and it remains very popular today among Catholics, Protestants, and non-believers. The cultural influences and exchanges that came about as a result of the medieval pilgrimages cannot be overestimated.

Saint Joan of Arc (May 30):- Patron Saint of France, Soldiers, Captives, and the Military (1412–1431)

Saint Joan of Arc was born in Domrémy (Alsace, France) to a family of peasants. At the age of thirteen she began to hear the voices of Saint Michael, Saint Catherine, and Saint Marguerite urging her to help Charles VII save France from the British. She did not answer these calls until she was seventeen, when she left home on horseback dressed as a knight to meet the future king of France, Charles VII, in Chinon, France. She carried a banner that had the Virgin of the Annunciation and an angel presenting the Virgin with a lily, the fleur-de-lys, the symbol of both the Virgin Mary and the French kings. Hers was a divine mission. Charles had an army assembled for her, and she led them into Orléans, where the French defeated the British. In 1429, Charles VII was crowned King of France. Unfortunately, after her victory, Joan of Arc endured fierce suffering. In 1430, she was captured by the Burgundians, allies of the British. She was accused of witchcraft, and in 1431 was tried by the Church and found guilty of heresy. She was burned alive at the stake in 1431 in Rouen at the age of nineteen. Her ashes were cast into the Seine River. Before dying she requested a cross. She kissed it and held it to her breast, and her last word was "Jesus." Her reputation was restored in 1456 but she was not canonized until 1920.

SAINT JACQUES

PRIEZ POUR NOUS

Early-1900s Saint James holy card. $6–$7.

Early-1900s Joan of Arc medals. $50–$65.

Original poster from WWI by Haskell Coffin showing Joan of Arc as an advertisement for war savings stamps. 18" × 28", $250–$300.

Early-1900s Joan of Arc postcard. $6–$7.

Early-1900s Joan of Arc medals. $50–$65.

Early-1900s Joan of Arc medals. $50–$65.

Saint John the Baptist (June 24): Patron Saint of Baptism, Lambs, and Monks (Died circa 32)

Saint John the Baptist was the cousin of Jesus. He lived and preached in the wilderness that people should repent because the kingdom of heaven was at hand. He baptized his followers in the river Jordan and baptized Christ himself. He hailed Christ as the Lamb of God and is often portrayed with a lamb. He was beheaded by Herod Antipas.

Saint Joseph (March 19): Patron Saint of Fathers, the Family, and the Home (First Century)

Joseph, a humble carpenter, was the husband of the Virgin Mary and the terrestrial father of Jesus. His veneration grew slowly until 1481 when Sixtus IV instituted his feast day. Often he is depicted as an old man holding Jesus as a child. In the sixteenth century, Saint Teresa of Avila helped spread his fame. In her autobiography she wrote how Joseph had helped cure her of an illness when she was twenty-six. In the United States there is a custom of burying a statue of Saint Joseph in the yard of a home to make it sell faster.

Early-1900s lithograph of John the Baptist as a child holding a symbolic lamb and cross. $25–$35.

Early-1900s tiny portable statues of Joseph in handmade metal cases. 1" tall, $30–$40 each.

Early-1900s Spanish painting of the Holy Family on tin with God and the Holy Spirit above. 10" × 14", $125–$150.

Early-1900s metal plaque of Joseph holding the Christ child, initialed by the engraver. 7½" × 9", $75–$85.

Early-1900s statue of Saint Joseph as an old man holding the Christ child. 18" tall, $145–$160.

Early-1900s statue of Saint Joseph with young Jesus. 18" tall, $145–$160.

Two early-1900s metal medallions showing Joseph and the Christ child, signed by the engraver. 6" in diameter, $65–$85 each.

Early-1900s holy cards with Saint Joseph. $6–$7 each.

Saint Jude (October 28): Patron Saint of Hopeless Situations (First Century)

The apostle Saint Jude is also called Thaddeus in the Gospels of Matthew and Mark, and is called Judas (not the traitor Judas Iscariot) in the Gospel of Luke and the Book of Acts. He is invoked in hopeless situations perhaps because the Epistle of Jude in the New Testament encourages the new Christians not to give up in the face of challenges from those who try to destroy the faith. He warns of "ungodly men, turning the grace of our God into lasciviousness, and denying the only Lord God, and our Lord Jesus Christ" (Verse 4). Jude is the voice of hope and encouragement in the face of adversity. He preached the gospel in the Middle East and later returned to Jerusalem in the year 62. Saint Bridgit of Sweden wrote about Saint Jude and caused him to be known as an advocate of desperate causes.

Saint Jude is a source of hope and inspiration to those who find themselves in great difficulty. Father James Tot, a member of the Cleretian Order, founded a shrine in Saint Jude's honor in Chicago. In 1929, many who suffered during the Great Depression of the 1930s visited the shrine. The world famous Saint Jude's Children's Hospital in Memphis, Tennessee, was founded by the late entertainer Danny Thomas in fulfillment of a vow made to the saint. After the Virgin of Guadalupe, San Judas Tadeo (Saint Jude Thaddeus) is the most revered holy person in Mexico and is very popular with the Mexican people who look to him for help.

1961 Mexican retablo, Rodolfo Rodríguez gives gratitude to Saint Jude Thaddeus for saving his life when a bus ran his car off the road in the Mexican mountains. 8" × 9½", $125–$150.

Contemporary holy card of Saint Jude. $6–$7.

Contemporary medal of Saint Jude. $15–$20.

Saint Luke (October 18): Patron Saint of Physicians, Surgeons, Writers and Artists (First Century)

1900s Guatemalan wood statue of Saint Luke with his ox. 7" tall, $100–$125.

Saint Luke was a physician who accompanied Saint Paul on his apostolic voyages. He is often portrayed with an ox because he begins the Book Of Luke writing about the animal sacrifice that Zacharias offered to the temple. A sixth-century legend represents him as a painter of the Virgin Mary.

Saint Mary Magdalene (July 22): Patron Saint of Penitents, Reformed Prostitutes, and Hairdressers (First Century)

Saint Mary Magdalene was from the town of Magdala on the western shore of the Sea of Galilee. She was the first witness of the Resurrection of Christ (Mark 16, Luke 10, John 20). A prostitute converted by Christ, she became His follower. She was present at the Crucifixion (John 19). Mary Magdalene is always portrayed with long hair and a jar of oil. In gratitude for the mercy of Jesus, she washed His feet and dried them with her hair, anointing them with oil. There are many different stories told about Mary Magdalene. According to Provençal tradition, after the Ascension of Christ to heaven, she was set adrift in a boat with two other women named Mary. These women, along with Lazarus, arrived in Provence and Mary Magdalene went to live on a hill called the Sainte Baume where she stayed until her death. The Sainte Baume is a popular pilgrimage site in France today.

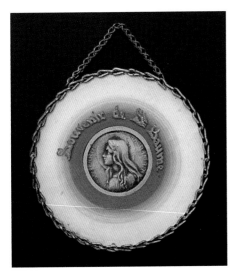

Early-1900s framed glass medallion of Saint Mary Magdalene. 4" in diameter, $50–$60.

Early-1900s Saint Mary Magdalene medal. $35–$40.

Early-1900s Saint Mary Magdalene holy card. $6–$7.

Saint Rita (May 22): Patron Saint of Impossible Causes and Smallpox (1381–1457)

Born in Italy, Saint Rita was married against her will to a mean and abusive man who was killed by his enemies. After her two sons died, she entered a convent where she suffered a serious illness. After she got well, she showed great kindness for sick members of her community. Her courageous suffering inspired others to seek her help with their own vicissitudes, and she helped desperate people and performed miracles during her lifetime. She had a wound on her forehead from wearing a crown of thorns to share Christ's suffering and pain.

Early-1900s Saint Rita holy card. $6–$7.

Saint Rose of Lima (August 23): Patron Saint of Latin America and the Philippines, Gardeners, and the Dominican Sisters (1586–1617)

Born in Lima, Peru, Saint Rose was the first saint canonized in the Americas. Saint Rose of Lima was born into a poor family of Spanish origin and had to work at humble jobs like selling roses from her garden to help support her family. She entered the third order of the Dominicans. She is often portrayed with roses and the Christ child. She lived her vows in a tiny cabin in the garden of the family home in a state of poverty and deprivation.

Early-1900s metal medallion of Saint Rose of Lima, patroness of the Americas. 4" in diameter, $65–$75.

Saint Sebastian (January 20): Patron Saint of Athletes, Archers, Policemen, and Those Suffering Plague (Third Century)

Saint Sebastian was a Pretorian guard in Rome in the service of Diocletian. He used his position to protect Christians. He was denounced and condemned to be shot to death by arrows. He miraculously survived and was cared for by Irene, the widow of a martyr. Since he survived the arrows that attacked his body and since plagues were attributed to the arrows of divine anger, he is invoked against the plague. After he was cured, he went to see Diocletian to reproach him for his cruelty to the Christians. The emperor had him whipped and sentenced him to death. His body was thrown into a sewer in Rome. He appeared to a Roman woman in a dream telling her where his body could be found and asking to be buried in the catacombs. His suffering and torment inspired numerous Renaissance artists, establishing the archetype of a handsome young man, nude and beautiful, covered with arrows.

Early-1900s colored lithograph of Saint Sebastian. 8" × 10", $25–$30.

Contemporary framed picture of Saint Sebastian. 4" × 6", $25–$30.

Saint Thérèse of Lisieux (October 3): Patron Saint of Missionaries (1873–1897)

Thérèse Martin is often called the "Little Flower." She is also known as Saint Thérèse of the Child Jesus and of the Holy Face. She became a Carmelite nun when she was only fifteen. She offered sacrifices to God in small ways, known as her "little way." In 1895 she began to show the first symptoms of tuberculosis. She suffered a great deal both spiritually and physically and died in 1897 at the age of twenty-four. Before she died she promised to "spend my heaven doing good on Earth" and "let fall a shower of roses." She wrote a book about her experiences called *The Story of a Soul*, which became an international best seller. There are many accounts of her miraculous healings and answering of prayers. There are also stories of the appearances of roses and their fragrance. She has had a profound impact on the faithful and is one of the most inspiring and popular saints.

Early-1900s marble plaque with image of Saint Thérèse. 3" × 3½", $75–$85.

Early-1900s holy card of Sainte Thérèse. $6–$7.

Early-1900s silver medals of Saint Thérèse. $35–$50 each.

CHAPTER FIVE
HOLY BEINGS

Images of holy beings have long been a component of religious devotion. They are of a personal nature and represent simple veneration and inspiration. They are visual reminders of faith in the home and are placed on a wall, a table, or a mantel, often in homes where there is very little other decoration. They are part of the lives of the people in the home and bring simple beauty and inspiration to those who see them every day. These images vary greatly in both subject and materials. They were often bought as souvenirs of a pilgrimage to shrines such as Lourdes, or were gifts from a voyage of a family member who went on a religious mission or pilgrimage. Many of these images were produced in the nineteenth century, and until the middle of the past century it was common to find them in Catholic homes, especially in rural areas. Today they are less common and seem to have fallen out of favor. These articles of faith from the past are symbols and sources of inspiration for practicing Catholics, not objects of worship.

Early-1900s free-standing religious articles. 2"–3½", $35 – 45 each.

Early-1900s framed motto *"Dieu Seul"* (God Alone). 10½" × 9", $75–$95.

Early-1900s Bakelite cradle cross with image of Jesus. 4" tall, $75–$95.

Late-1800s Mexican painting of the Virgin Mary on tin. 9" × 11", $175–$195.

Early-1900s holy water bottles from the shrine of Lourdes. 8½"–11" tall, $45–$55 each.

Early-1900s statue of Jesus. 12" tall, $125–$150.

Early-1900s meerschaum carvings of Christ under glass. 2½"–3" tall, $125–$145 each.

Likenesses of holy people take many forms in popular sacred art. Usually these articles were simple and were produced for the faithful of modest means. Statuettes of all types and materials were set on a mantel, a bedside table, a shelf, or inside a cabinet. They were usually small and unassuming and were made from bronze, iron, copper, or a mixture of metals. Ceramic statues were very popular, and the famous faience houses produced religious statues as well as plates, platters, and tureens. Sometimes the figures were carved from wood or limestone or produced in porcelain, glass, plaster, enamel, and even plastic. They usually represent saints, the Virgin Mary, or Jesus. Framed pictures or portraits of holy people were also popular. Metal plaques with the images of sacred people were also hung on walls or over the fireplaces of the home.

Early-1900s marble plaque with bronze figure of Jesus. 4" tall, $65–$75.

Napoleon III blue velvet crucifix with elaborate carved Passion instruments and crown of thorns. 15½" tall, $150–$175.

Early-1900s free-standing copper holy water font surrounded by fleur-de-lys. 4" tall, $125–$135.

Early-1900s Greek Orthodox bronze picture of the Virgin Mary and Christ child with intricate filigree frame. 9" × 9", $150–$175.

Early-1900s silver medal of Jesus wearing a crown of thorns. $45–$50.

Early-1900s small enamel religious medals. $75–$95 each.

One of the most popular examples of homage to holy people is the extensive production of religious medals, still very popular today. These medals sometimes have names and dates engraved on the back. The quality and beauty of these older medals is outstanding. They are made from gold or gold plate, silver, bronze, or a mixture of metals. These medals are sometimes made into pins and rings or are added to rosaries to commemorate a pilgrimage or special occasion. Medals are worn around the neck for protection from harm, for safety, as devotion to a special saint, Jesus Christ or the Virgin Mary, or as a memento of a special event such as the First Communion.

Contemporary crucifix in a shrine. 10" tall, $45–$55.

Early-1900s cross with the Holy Face of Jesus in the center. $55–$65.

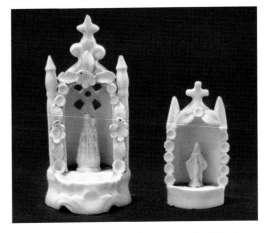

Early-1900s porcelain shrines to the Virgin Mary with holy water fonts, surrounded by flowers. 4"–4½" tall, $85–$100 each.

Early-1900s brass book with pictures of Lourdes, worn as a pendant. 1" × 1½", $95–$125.

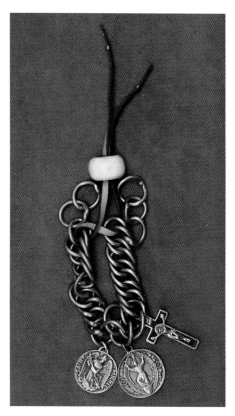

Early-1900s rosary bracelets with religious medals. $75–$100.

Contemporary bracelets made from heavy chain, two medals, and a crucifix. $175–$195.

The Virgin Mary

Saint Mary or the Blessed Virgin Mary is identified in the Bible as the Mother of Jesus Christ. Very little is known about her life. She was born to Anne and Joachim and promised in marriage to Joseph, a carpenter. She was of the lineage of King David. The story of Mary is told in the Gospel of Luke. The angel Gabriel appeared to her and announced that she had been chosen by God to give birth to the promised Messiah. An angel also appeared to Joseph in a dream and told him not to be afraid to take Mary as a wife "for that which is conceived in her is of the Holy Ghost" (Matthew 1:20). Mary and Joseph had to travel to Bethlehem for a census. There was no place to stay except a stable, and Jesus was born in a manger in Bethlehem.

The Blessed Virgin Mary has been venerated since the early days of Christianity. As a maternal figure of love and kindness she is revered all over the world. She is one of the most holy people in the Catholic Church. Her image appears on a myriad of personal religious objects, and she occupies an important place in churches, cathedrals, and religious art.

Early-1900s oil on canvas portrait of the Virgin Mary with angels. 19½" × 26", $150–$195.

Early-1900s ex-voto on convex glass with an image of Mary and gold letters in the background. 4" × 4½", $85–$95.

Early-1900s copper medallion showing the Virgin Mary and Christ Child. 5" in diameter, $60–$70.

Early-1900s pewter image of the Virgin Mary surrounded by lilies and stars in the nimbus, signed by the engraver. 9" in diameter, $100–$125.

Early-1900s portrait of the Virgin Mary on enamel with gold frame made into a brooch. 1½"–2", $100–$125.

Early-1900s meerschaum carving of the Virgin Mary under convex glass. 3" in diameter, $100–$135.

Early-1900s oil on canvas portrait of the Virgin Mary with angels. 19½" × 26", $150–$195.

Early-1900s copper medallions, one with an image of Mary and the other with a monogram of the Virgin Mary, initialed by the engraver. Both 5" × 7", $85–$95 each.

Early-1900s wood plaque with metal image of the Virgin Mary and Christ child. 5½" × 7½", $75–$85.

Early-1900s portrait of the Virgin Mary with fancy tin frame. 2½" × 4", $85–$95.

Early-1900s framed portrait of the Virgin Mary. 3½" × 5", 85–$95.

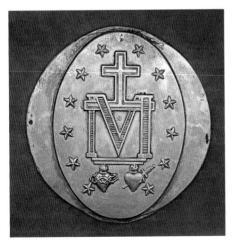

Early-1900s copper medallion with monogram of the Virgin Mary. 5½" in diameter, $45–$55.

Apparitions of the Virgin

The Virgin Mary has appeared in many places over the centuries, often to very humble people, and is one of the most important subjects of sacred art. On objects of devotion, besides her monograms of the letters of M, MA, and A.M.R. (Ave Maria Regina), we often see symbols that represent her, such as a pierced heart, the lily, the fleur-de-lys, the lily of the valley, the rose, and the star. We focus here on only a few of these Marian apparitions, chosen for their importance in the country of their appearance and for Catholics all over the world as well.

Early-1900s etched glass pieces with monogram of the Virgin Mary. Approximately 2" tall, $35–$40 each.

Detail of early-1900s hand-painted velvet altar cloth with rose symbol and monogram of the Virgin Mary. $300–$350.

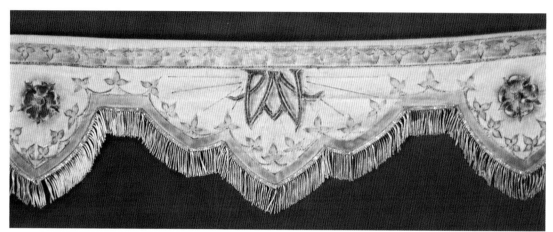

The Virgin of Guadalupe of Mexico (December 12)

The beloved patron saint of Mexico appeared to Juan Diego, a humble peasant, on Tepeyac Hill, outside of Mexico City in 1531. She asked him to have a church built in her honor and to make her request known to the bishop at Tenochtitlán. The bishop wanted a sign that she had indeed appeared to this humble man. In another appearance, she instructed Juan Diego to go to the top of the hill and cut some flowers and bring them to her. He did as she asked and cut some red roses and wrapped them in his cloak, or tilma. He then went again to visit the bishop. This time the bishop believed him because when he opened his tilma to let the flowers fall out there was a beautiful image of the Blessed Virgin Mary just as he had described her. When Juan Diego returned to his village, he found his sick uncle, Juan Bernardino, had

Early-1900s gold-plated medal of the Virgin of Guadalupe. $55–$65.

been cured. Juan Bernardino told Juan Diego that a young woman had appeared to him and told him that she had sent his nephew to Tenochtitlán with a picture of herself. She had told Juan Bernardino to call her Santa Maria de Guadalupe. Today a very large cathedral, which will hold up to ten thousand worshippers, has been built near the site where the Virgin of Guadalupe first appeared to Juan Diego. The cape of the humble peasant with the Virgin's picture is on display in this most popular pilgrimage site in the Western Hemisphere. The Virgin of Guadalupe is always portrayed with an aureole, the elongated nimbus that surrounds the whole body.

The Virgin of Caridad del Cobre of Cuba (September 8)

According to tradition, around 1612, three young boys were in a boat floating in the rough seas in the Nipe Bay of northeastern Cuba when they saw something white appear over the top of the waves. As they got closer, they saw it was the Virgin Mary holding the baby Jesus in her arms. They saw that her clothes were not wet and she was standing on a wooden plaque that said *"Yo soy la Virgen de la Caridad,"* which means "I am the Virgin of Charity." Two of the boys were brothers named Rodrigo and Juan de Hoyos and the third was a ten-year-old Afro-Cuban child, Juan Moreno. They are known as the "Three Johns" (*los tres Juanes*). They took the statue to El Cobre, a copper mining town nearby, and there a shrine was constructed in her honor. According to tradition, the Virgin was an Afro-Cuban and the child was white. The beloved Virgin of Caridad is nicknamed Cachita by the Cuban people. She even made an appearance in Hemingway's novel *The Old Man and the Sea*. The fisherman in the story promised to make a pilgrimage to the shrine of the Virgin de Caridad if he caught a fish.

She is venerated by the followers of Santeria, an Afro-Cuban religion that is a fusion of Catholicism and the African Yoruba religion. In Santeria, the Virgin is associated with Oshun, the Yoruba goddess of love and femininity.

Both Oshun and the Virgin de Caridad are represented by the color yellow. Cubans show their devotion to her by placing sunflowers on her altar and by offering her special treats like honey. Because of her mixed race, the Virgin de Caridad del Cobre symbolizes the Cuban people. When Castro became ill a few years ago, many of his followers made a pilgrimage to her basilica to pray for his return to good health. She also has an important following in the United States among Cuban exiles and there is a church devoted to her facing Biscayne Bay in Miami. A large celebration is held for her on September 8 in Miami and is attended by thousands of followers each year. Cachita is alive and well in Cuba after 400 years.

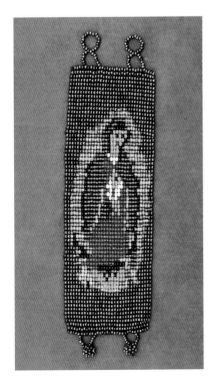

Contemporary Mexican handmade beaded bracelet with the Virgin of Guadalupe. $10–$15.

Image showing the Virgin of Caridad, patron saint of Cuba, with message: "Mother of Cuba, 400 years with us."

1900s statue of the Virgin of Caridad in Havana, Cuba.

Our Lady of Fatima (1917)

In 1916 an angel appeared to three children who were taking care of their sheep near their home in Fatima, Portugal. The three children were Lucia Santos and her cousins Jacinta and Francisco Marto. The angel visited them three times. On May 13, 1917, the Virgin Mary appeared to them surrounded by a brightly shining light. After that she had other apparitions, always on the thirteenth of the month. She made her last apparition to the children on October 13, 1917.

At the last apparition there occurred the "Miracle of the Sun," in which the sun was surrounded by bright colors similar to those in a stained-glass window and seemed to be whirling and moving toward the earth. The Virgin revealed to Lucia Santos three secrets that were predictions of events that would occur in Europe, one of which was the demise of communism. These predictions have all come to pass according to interpretations by the faithful and the Catholic Church.

Early-1900s picture of the Virgin of Fatima with elaborate silver frame. $95–$115.

Contemporary small images of the Virgin of Fatima. $25–$35 each.

Contemporary wood plaque with image of the Virgin of Fatima and a crucifix. 3" × 5½", $35–$45.

The Lord Jesus Christ

The name Jesus is derived from Hebrew for "God saves" or Savior. His title of Christ comes from the Greek equivalent of the Hebrew word "Messiah," which means "the anointed one." There was a custom in Israel of anointing kings, priests and prophets with oil. According to His followers, Jesus Christ was destined to become the long promised Messiah, the King of Kings. Christians believe that Jesus is the Son of God and part of the Holy Trinity. According to Christian beliefs, Jesus came to Earth in human form and was born to the Virgin Mary and to Joseph, a carpenter in Nazareth, His Earthly father. His life and death were dedicated to the redemption of mankind. In the book of Matthew, 20:28, Jesus said to Peter: "The Son of Man did not come to be served but to give his life as a ransom for many." Jesus died to save all men and women from their sins. Through His death and resurrection, Jesus opened heaven to all who would follow Him (John 3:16). After His crucifixion, Christ arose from the dead, victorious over death. His life on Earth was brief—only thirty-three years.

Early-1900s portrait of Jesus with gold frame, made into a brooch. 2" tall, $85–$115.

Early-1900s meerschaum carved figure of Jesus. 2" × 2½", $95–$125.

Early-1900s limestone carved face of Jesus with crown of thorns. 4½" × 4½", $100–$125.

Early-1900s framed medallion of Jesus. 3" × 4", $75–$85.

Early-1900s Jerusalem mother of pearl and marquetry crucifixes with the stations of the cross. 5½" tall, $75–$95.

Early-1900s portrait of Jesus with fancy tin frame. 2½" × 4", $85–$95.

Early-1900s Sacred Heart medals. $55–$65 each.

Early-1900s framed marble crucifix. 5" × 6", $100–$125.

Early-1900s embroidered figure of Jesus mounted on a red velvet plaque. 8" × 13½", $90–$100.

Early-1900s framed Sacred Heart surrounded by a gold crown of thorns and passion symbols. 5½" × 8", $100–$125.

The figure of Jesus has been represented by his followers over the centuries in art, devotional objects, architecture, and almost any religious display one can imagine. There are a multitude of symbols for Christ but we will examine only a few that are recognized by Catholics everywhere. One example is the pelican feeding her young with her own blood. This is one of the most widely used and dramatic symbols of the Lord's Atonement. It is said that in times of famine the pelican tears open her own breast to give her blood as nourishment to her young, just as Christ sacrificed his own life so we, his children, could live. Another example is the *Agnus Dei* or Lamb of God. This symbol tells the story of man's sin and the sacrifice of the lamb who is Christ and who was sacrificed for us on the cross. The lamb has a crown over his head that represents a symbol of holiness and divinity. The butterfly represents the three stages of eternal life, given to us by Christ through his sacrifice. The larva is mortal man; the chrysalis is the grave; and the last stage is the pupa that breaks its shell and flies toward the heavens just as man is able to go to heaven because Christ died to give us eternal life. The dual nature of the mermaid, who is part woman and part fish, is a symbol of the duality of Christ; he is divine and human. The daisy represents the freshness and innocence of the Christ child. Christ is also the good shepherd who lovingly cares for his flock. He is often seen as a young man carrying a lamb over his shoulders.

In addition to the many symbols of Christ, there are also holy monograms. IHC sometimes written IHS or even JHS, is the abbreviation of the Greek work IHCOYC, which stands for Jesus. Sometimes the Greek letters Alpha and Omega are used to designate Christ, who is the beginning and end of all things. It was combined with the Chi Rho symbols in the ancient catacombs. The letters I.N.R.I. are often written over the head of Christ on the crucifix and stand for *Iesus Nazarenus Rex Iudaeorum*, or Jesus of Nazareth, King of the Jews.

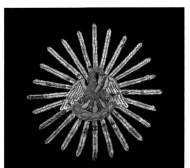

Early-1900s detail of the pelican symbol of Jesus from the cape of a chasuble. $300–$350.

Early-1900s intricate bead work picture with the pelican symbol holding a cross. 4" × 4", $85–$95.

Early-1900s needlepoint fragment of *Agnus Dei* (Lamb of God). 12" × 6", $65–$75.

Early-1900s holy card with Jesus. $6–$7.

Early-1900s medallion of Jesus in a
bronze frame. 1¼" × 2", $45–$55.

Early-1900s detail of IHS emblem on
velvet chasuble. $350–$400.

Early-1900s
holy card of
Jesus and his
cousin John
the Baptist as
children with
symbolic lamb.
$6–$7.

Early-1900s
silver medal
signed by the
engraver and
fragment from
an ecclesiastical
garment with
stumpwork and
sequins, both
with the Lamb
of God symbol.
$55–$65 each.

Early-1900s bronze statue of Jesus. 6" tall,
$85–$95.

Early-1900s brass crucifix with angel faces on the ends of the cross. 5" tall, $75–$95.

Contemporary example of the tau crucifix. 3" tall, $40–$50.

Late-1800s bronze crucifix on a stand, fleur-de-lys at the ends of the cross and skull and crossbones at the base. 7½" tall, $95–$125.

Early-1900s Sacred Heart holy
cards. $6–$7 each.

Early-1900s silver Sacred Heart
medals. $50–$60.

Early-1900s bronze medallion
of Jesus, initialed by the
engraver. 7" in diameter.
$75–$85.

The Divine Infant Jesus of Prague

Veneration of the baby Jesus began in the Middle Ages. The first small statues were made of wax. One of the most famous of these images is the Divine Infant Jesus of Prague. The original statue of the Infant Jesus of Prague was made from painted wax and was given by Princess Polixene de Lobkowitz in 1628 to the Carmelite convent in Prague to obtain the protection of Jesus during the devastating religious wars in Prague. Devotion to this statue spread all over Bohemia (Baudoin, 150). The child Jesus wears a flared robe that is richly adorned and holds a globe with a cross above it in his left hand. He wears a crown. The right hand is lifted in a gesture of blessing with two fingers raised.

Early-1900s holy cards with Jesus as a child. $6–$7 each.

Early-1900s statue of the Infant of Prague. 12½" tall, $150–$175.

Early-1900s pewter statue of the Infant of Prague. 6" tall, $100–$125.

The Angels

The holy angels are heavenly beings with origins in the Old Testament. The traditional representation of angels has been beautiful, blonde female creatures with dove-like wings. However there are all kinds of angels who are the protectors of mankind; they are our guardian angels. Angels are a much loved theme in religious art and were frequently portrayed in early paintings and sculptures. They are also very popular today. The three archangels, Saint Michael, Saint Gabriel, and Saint Raphael, have human bodies with wings. They are mentioned in both the Old Testament and the New Testament. All three archangels are celebrated on September 29.

1600s fragment from the border of a Flemish tapestry. 15" × 9", $250–$275.

1700s silk embroidered angel; fragment from a religious banner. 13" tall, $150–$195.

Early-1900s faience angel holy water font. 14" tall, $225–$275.

Early-1900s brass angel medallion, signed by the engraver. 6½" in diameter, $95–$125.

Early-1900s brass angel. 3½" tall, $75–$85.

Early-1900s brass angel medallions, initialed by the engraver. 7" and 5" in diameter, $85–$125.

Saint Michael is usually portrayed in sacred art holding a sword and standing triumphantly over a slain dragon, symbol of the devil. He is the protector of Christians and the Church against their enemies. His name means "Who Is Like God" or *Ut Quis Deus* in Latin. According to legend he appeared several times in history answering the prayers of those who were in trouble. His voice was one of those heavenly voices heard by Joan of Arc urging her to save France from the English. It is said that at the hour of death he guides the soul to God. His most famous shrine is Mont Saint Michel in Normandy. Saint Michael is the patron saint of soldiers, police officers, and radiologists.

Saint Gabriel was the messenger of the Annunciation. He was sent by God to announce to Mary that she would give birth to a son who would be Jesus. His name means "man of God" or "God is my strength." He is the angel of the Judgment Day and holds a trumpet. Saint Gabriel is the patron saint of communication workers.

Saint Raphael is the chief of the guardian angels. He appears in the book of Tobit and his name means "God heals." He cured the father of Tobias of his blindness. Saint Raphael is the patron saint of doctors, shepherds, and voyagers.

Art deco pewter plaque of Saint Gabriel and the Virgin Mary, signed by the engraver. 7" in diameter, $75–$95.

Early-1900s fragments from a religious banner representing Saint Michael, whose name means "Who is Like God" (*Quis Ut Deus*), in gold stumpwork. Also in gold stumpwork are the words *"Protégez la France"* (Protect France). $350–$450 for the two.

Early-1900s copper plaque of Saint Raphael with Tobias, whose father he cured using an organ of a fish. 7½" in diameter, $95–$115.

Early-1900s embroidered figure of Saint Michael slaying the dragon. 24" tall, $225–$250.

Early-1900s medals of Saint Michael. $45–$55 each.

Selected List of Popular Patron Saints Sorted by Name

Here are some of the most popular patron saints sorted by name, followed by the professions or people they represent and their feast date.

A

Andrew: fishermen; November 30
Anne: grandmothers, librarians, lace-makers, homemakers; July 26
Anthony of Padua: people seeking lost items or people; June 13
Appolonia: dentists, toothaches; February 9

B

Barbara: miners, artillerymen, builders, mathematicians; December 4.
Benedict of Nursia: farmers, monks; April 4
Bernadette of Lourdes: shepherds, shepherdesses, the ill; April 16
Blaise: veterinarians, weavers; February 3

C

Catherine Labouré: Miraculous Medal; December 30
Cecilia: musicians; November 22
Christopher: travelers, drivers, pilots; July 25

D

Damian: doctors; September 26
Dymphna: mental health professionals; May 15

E

Eligius: jewelers, goldsmiths, blacksmiths; December 1

F

Fiacre: gardeners, taxi drivers; August 30
Florian: firefighters; May 4
Francis of Assisi: animals; October 4

G

Gabriel the Archangel: communications workers; September 29
George: equestrians, butchers, soldiers; April 23

H

Honorius of Amiens: bakers, pastry chefs; May 16

I

Isidore of Madrid: farmers, manual laborers; May 15

J

James: equestrians, pilgrims; July 25
Jerome: librarians, translators; September 30
Joan of Arc: soldiers, Girl Scouts; May 30
Joseph: carpenters, craftsmen; March 19
Jude (Jude Thaddeus): impossible causes, police officers; October 28
Julian the Hospitaller: boatmen, travelers; January 27

L

Lawrence: tanners, cooks, librarians; August 10
Luke: doctors, artists; October 18

M

Mary Magdalene: hairdressers, pharmacists; July 22
Martin de Porres: mixed race people, lottery winners, and public education; November 3
Matthew: accountants, bankers; May 14
Michael the Archangel: radiologists, soldiers, police officers; September 29

P

Patrick: engineers; March 17

R

Raphael the Archangel: doctors, shepherds, voyagers; September 29
Rita: impossible or desperate causes, smallpox; May 22
Roch: surgeons, second-hand dealers; August 16
Rose of Lima: gardeners, embroiderers; August 23

S

Sebastian: athletes, archers; January 20

T

Thérèse de Lisieux: missionaries, florists; October 1
Teresa de Avila: headaches, checkers players; October 15
Thomas Aquinas: students, teachers, universities; January 28

V

Valentine: lovers; February 14
Veronica: photographers; February 4

SELECTED LIST OF POPULAR PATRON SAINTS SORTED BY PROFESSION

Here are some of the most popular patron saints sorted by profession, followed by their name and their feast date.

A

Accountants: Matthew, May 14
Animals: Francis of Assisi, October 4
Archers: Sebastian, January 20
Artillerymen: Barbara, December 4
Artists: Luke, October 18
Athletes: Sebastian, January 20

B

Bakers: Honorius of Amiens, May 16
Bankers: Matthew, May 14
Blacksmiths: Eligius, December 1
Boatmen: Julian the Hospitaller, January 27
Builders: Barbara, December 4
Butchers: George, April 23

C

Carpenters: Joseph, March 19
Checkers players: Teresa de Avila, October 15
Communications: Gabriel the Archangel, September 29
Cooks: Lawrence, August 10
Craftsmen: Joseph, March 19

D

Dentists: Appolonia, February 9
Desperate causes: Rita, May 22
Doctors: Damian, September 26; Luke, October 18; Raphael the Archangel, September 29
Drivers: Christopher, July 25

E

Embroiderers: Rose of Lima, August 23
Engineers: Patrick, March 17
Equestrians: George, April 23: James, July 25
Equestrians,

F

Farmers: Benedict of Nursia, April 4; Isidore of Madrid, May 15
Firefighters: Florian, May 4
Fisherman: Andrew, November 30
Florists: Thérèse de Lisieux, October 1

G

Gardeners: Fiacre, August 30; Rose of Lima, August 23
Girl Scouts: Joan of Arc, May 30
Goldsmiths: Eligius, December 1
Grandmothers: Anne, July 26

H

Hairdressers: Mary Magdalene, July 22
Headaches: Teresa de Avila , October 15
Homemakers: Anne, July 26

I

Ill people: Bernadette of Lourdes, April 16
Impossible causes: Jude (Jude Thaddeus), October 28; Rita, May 22

J

Jewelers: Eligius, December 1

L

Law-makers: Anne, July 26
Librarians, Anne, July 26; Jerome, September 30; Lawrence, August 10
Lottery winners: Martin de Porres, November 3
Lovers: Valentine, February 14

M

Manual laborers: Isidore of Madrid, May 15
Mathematicians: Barbara, December 4
Mental health professionals: Dymphna, May 15
Miners: Barbara, December 4
Miraculous Medal: Catherine Labouré, December 30
Missionaries: Thérèse de Lisieux, October 1
Mixed race people: Martin de Porres, November 3
Monks: Benedict of Nursia, April 4
Musicians: Cecilia, November 22

P

Pastry chefs: Honorius of Amiens, May 16
People seeking lost items or people: Anthony of Padua, June 13
Pharmacists: Mary Magdalene, July 22
Photographers: Veronica, February 4
Pilgrims: James, July 25
Pilots: Christopher, July 25
Police officers: Jude (Jude Thaddeus), October 28; Michael the Archangel, September 29
Public education: Martin de Porres, November 3

R

Radiologists: Michael the Archangel, September 29

S

Second-hand dealers: Roch, August 16
Shepherdesses: Bernadette of Lourdes, April 16
Shepherds: Bernadette of Lourdes, April 16; Raphael the Archangel, September 29
Smallpox: Rita, May 22
Soldiers: George, April 23; Joan of Arc, May 30; Michael the Archangel, September 29
Students: Thomas Aquinas, January 28
Surgeons: Roch, August 16

T

Tanners: Lawrence, August 10
Taxi drivers: Fiacre, August 30
Teachers: Thomas Aquinas, January 28
Toothaches: Appolonia, February 9
Translators: Jerome, September 30
Travelers: Christopher, July 25; Julian the Hospitaller, January 27

U

Universities: Thomas Aquinas, January 28

V

Veterinarians: Blaise, February 3
Voyagers: Raphael the Archangel, September 29

W

Weavers: Blaise, February 3
Workers: Gabriel the Archangel, September 29

SELECTED BIBLIOGRAPHY

Alger, William. *History of the Cross*. Boston: American Unitarian Association, 1858.

Arbeteta Mira, Letizia. "El exvoto de Hernán Cortés." *Dones y promesas: 500 años de arte ofrenda (exvotos mexicanos)*. Mexico City: Mexico, D.F.: Centro Cultural/Arte Contemporáneo, Fundación Cultural Televisa, 1996, 234–40.

Baudoin, Jacques. *Grand livre des saints: Culte et iconographie en Occident*. Nonette, France: Éditions Créer, 1993.

Berthod, Bernard, and Elizabeth Hardouin-Fugier. *Dictionnaire des objets de dévotion dans l'Europe catholique*. Paris: Les Éditions de l'Amateur, 2006.

Calamari, Barbara, and Sandra Di Pasqua. *Holy Cards*. New York: Harry N. Abrams, Inc., 2004.

Daix, Georges. *Dictionnaire des saints*. France: Éditions Jean-Claude Lattès, 1996.

Daubier, Jean. *Le Grand Livre des Médailles Miraculeuses*. Paris: Éditions Trajectoire, 1998.

Durand, Jorge. *Los Exvotos: vida y milagros de los mexicanos*. San Luis Potosí, Mexico: Cuadernos del Centro Serie Divulgación, 1995.

Finley, Mitch. *The Patron Saints Handbook*. Ijamsville, Maryland: The Word Among Us Press, 2010.

Kotowicz, Juliette. "Leur culte sur la commode." *Aladin*, July 2009, 50–55.

Ladame, Jean. *Les saints de la piété populaire*. Paris: Éditions S.O.S., 1985.

Landsberg, Jacques de. *L'Art en croix: le thème de la crucifixion dans l'histoire de l'art*. Tournai, Belgium: La Renaissance du Livre, 2001.

Lejeune, René. *Rosaire traditionnel et rosaire biblique*. Paris: Éditions Saint-Paul, 1987.

Marucchi, Orazio. "Archaeology of the Cross and Crucifix," *The Catholic Encyclopedia* 4 (1908), http://www.newadvent.org/cathen/04517a.htm.

Medina San Román, María del Carmen. "Votive Art: Miracles of Two Thousand Years," *Folk Art of Spain and the Americas: El Alma del Pueblo*. Edited by Marion Oettinzer, Jr., 106–127, New York: San Antonio Museum of Art, 1997.

Pierrard, Pierre. *Dictionnaire des prénoms et des saints*. Paris: Larousse, 1998.

Rodríguez Becerra, Salvador. "Formas de la religiosidad popular, el exvoto, su valor histórico y etnográfico." Edited by María Jesús Buxó. *La religiosidad popular*, Vol. 1. Barcelona: Antropos, 1989, 123–142.

Rodríguez Becerra, Salvador, and José María Vázquez Soto. *Ex-votos de Andalucía: Milagros y promesas en la religiosidad popular*. Seville: Argantonio, Ediciones Andaluzas, 1980.

Ricard, Robert. *The Spiritual Conquest of Mexico: An Essay on the Apostolate and the Evangelizing Methods of the Mendicant Orders in New Spain: 1523–1572*. Translated by Lesley Byrd Simpson. Berkeley: University of California Press, 1966.

Stampfler, Anne. *Les chapelets: Objets de culte, objets de collection*. Chapetière, France: Éditions des Monts d'Auvergne, 2011.

Thurston, Herbert. "Missal." *The Catholic Encyclopedia* Vol. 10. New York: Robert Appleton Company, 1911. 2 Nov. 2013, http://www.newadvent.org/cathen/10354c.htm.

Thurston, Herbert, and Andrew Shipman. "The Rosary," *The Catholic Encyclopedia* Vol. 13. New York: Robert Appleton Company, 1912. 1 Aug. 2013, http://www.newadvent.org/cathen/13184b.htm.

Ward, Henry Dana. *History of the Cross: The Pagan Origin and Idolatrous Adoption and Worship of the Image*. Philadelphia: Claxston, Remsen & Haffelfinger, 1871.

Webber, F. R. *Church Symbolism: An Explanation of the More Important Symbols of the Old and New Testament, the Primitive, the Medieval, and the Modern Church*. Detroit: Gale Research Company, 1971. First published 1938 by J. H. Jansen.

Woodward, Kenneth L. *Making Saints: How the Catholic Church Determines Who becomes a Saint, Who Doesn't and Why*. New York: Simon and Schuster, 1990.

Worth, William. "Miraculous Images and Living Saints in Mexican Folk Catholicism," *Folk Art of Spain and the Americas: El Alma del Pueblo*. Edited by Marion Oettinzer, Jr. New York: San Antonio Museum of Art, 1997, 159–189.

INDEX

June K. Laval, PhD, is professor of French and
Spanish at Kennesaw State University in Atlanta,
Georgia. During her travels to France and Latin America,
she became interested in vintage religious objects and
over the last decade has used her knowledge of the
French and Spanish languages and cultures as well as
her academic training to turn her passion for religious
articles used by everyday people into a rich collection.
When she is not involved with her academic work, you
can find June somewhere in France or Latin America,
shopping at local markets to enrich her collection, or in
the Périgord, France, where she and her husband
Philippe enjoy spending time in the village of Le
Recours in an old house they have restored.